Conditioning My Spirit

B Lynn Davis

WESTBOW
P R E S S®
A DIVISION OF THOMAS NELSON
& ZONDERVAN

WestBow Press books may be ordered through booksellers or by contacting:

WestBow Press
A Division of Thomas Nelson & Zondervan
1663 Liberty Drive
Bloomington, IN 47403
www.westbowpress.com
1 (866) 928-1240

ISBN: 978-1-5127-6497-0 (sc)
ISBN: 978-1-5127-6496-3 (e)

Library of Congress Control Number: 2016919402

Print information available on the last page.

WestBow Press rev. date: 12/6/2016

To God be the glory

Introduction

> Then Nadab and Abihu, the sons of Aaron, each
> took his censer and put fire in it, put incense on it,
> and offered profane fire before the LORD, which
> He had not commanded them. So fire went out
> from the LORD and devoured them, and they
> died before the LORD. And Moses said to Aaron,
> "This is what the LORD spoke, saying: 'By those
> who come near Me I must be regarded as holy;
> And before all the people I must be glorified.'" So
> Aaron held his peace. (Leviticus 10:1–3 NKJV)

Do you believe that the standards of God regarding his people
have changed over the last few thousands of years? Or perhaps
his expectations of those who are called by his name have been
modified to accommodate modern civilization? Unless God has
changed, the same requirement stands firm forever. In Malachi
3:6 (NIV) he says, "I the LORD do not change." God still must
be regarded as holy, and he still wants all the glory. Nadab and
Abihu were sons of Aaron and served as priests in the house of
God. These were men who handled God's day-to-day affairs

on earth. But one day they got ahead of themselves and did something outside of God's command to them, which resulted in their deaths. Just like Nadab and Abihu, you and I are called to handle God's day-to-day business on earth. One day you and I will hear the words, "Time's up." Are you ready to face God? Are you prepared to leave this world behind without any regrets? It does not matter whether you have accomplished all the things in life that you wanted to do. Nor does it matter if you have not done all the things you intended to do for God. What matters is how you have spent your time here on earth after you gave your life to Jesus.

Right now we spend most of our time living like Nadab and Abihu did (on that one fateful day), assuming that how we do things is always the right way to do it. As Christians, there are many things we continually do that are contrary to the word of God. In Mark 12:31, we are told to love our neighbors as we love ourselves. Do we? Ephesians 6:12 says our fight is not against flesh and blood. Who are you fighting against? In Hebrew 13:5, we are to keep our lives free from the love of money and to be content with what we have. Are we? How about not judging others by their outward appearance (John 7:24)? In 1 John 2:15 we are asked not to love this world. Do we? Then there are the things we do base on traditions that may or may not have anything to do with God. These are traditions like wearing green on St. Patrick's Day, coloring eggs for Easter, or decorating a tree at Christmastime, or even things not associated with holidays, like washing our hands before each meal. Not that any of these things are bad in themselves. The problem is we tend to keep up a tradition, just because it has always been done this way. Most of them we do not know how they got started in the first place (Luke 11:37–38). Once Jesus was invited to a Pharisee's home for dinner and did not wash his hands before eating. The Pharisee was astonished by the fact the Jesus did not first wash his hands. Jesus said in Matthew 15:20 (NIV), "These are what defile a person; but eating with unwashed hands does not defile them." Jesus came to set us free from the traditions of men.

Do you know that there is nothing traditional about God? He alone is the standard, the Creator of the universe. Therefore, nothing has been passed down to him. God has no forefathers; he is the forerunner of life. Thank God for his grace, lest we would be consumed as Aaron's sons were. As believers in Christ, we must find out what God expects from us. Without wavering or compromising what we believe, let us enter into a relationship with God that will last for all eternity.

This book, *Conditioning My Spirit,* is written to the one who no longer wants to assume that they are in right standing with God, but to understand why they are in such a privileged position. It is about setting the reset button of your life in Christ and starting all over again. It expounds on how to turn your heart to God and live your life on earth as a new creature in an earthly body. It was written to teach us how to stop praying worthless prayers and to know without a doubt God is listening to us. Let's face it; it is not enough to call ourselves Christians and attend church, for it has lured many of us into a deep spiritual coma. We somehow think that as long as we hold on to his name, we can offer worthless sacrifices like Nadab and Abihu.

The most powerful part of a person is his or her spirit when it has become alive. It is often neglected and pushed aside to satisfy the flesh. Matthew 5:14 (NIV) says, "You are the light of the world." If we choose to forsake our spirit man within, then the light inside of us cannot shine as God intended it to do. Therefore, the good that God would have us to do will get lost in all the wrong we find ourselves involved in. Sadly, most of the things God would have us to do are never realized because we fail to follow his lead in our lives.

To operate in the earth as a spiritual being sometimes requires us to forfeit our hopes and dreams that center around our earthly desires. As new creatures in Christ, we have an obligation to answer God's call and stay on the pathway he has chosen for us. We cannot simultaneously be red hot for God while pursuing our earthly desires. Abandoning yourself to the one who died for your sins means you are to think less of the things of this world as being your true source of living. We must also be prepared to lose the support of the world since the world only loves its own. It is just as well since we are the product of the Lord Jesus Christ, our true source of living.

In 2 Kings 9, the eunuchs of wicked Jezebel were encouraged by Jehu (God's newly appointed king over Israel) to throw her down into the street, to which some of them complied. *Conditioning My Spirit* was written to encourage believers in Christ to overthrow the enemy out of their minds. As born-again believers, we are to follow the lead of the Holy Spirit and renounce every evil way in our hearts and minds. We must also remove all doubt about

God's requirement for our life and turn ourselves over to him to become like Jesus.

> Therefore, since we are receiving a kingdom which cannot be shaken, let us have grace, by which we may serve God acceptably with reverence and godly fear. For our God is a consuming fire. (Hebrew 12:28–29 NKJV)

I pray that your eyes and ears be open as mine were in writing this book.

Chapter 1

From Justification to Righteousness

> He did not enter by means of the blood of goats and calves; but he entered the Most Holy Place once for all by his own blood, thus obtaining eternal redemption. (Hebrews 9:12 NIV)

I read once that a pint of human blood has the potential to save at least three lives when separated into the main components: red cells, platelets, and plasma. The donated blood must be used as soon as possible to maintain its effectiveness. The average storage life is about six weeks before it loses its effectiveness. The handling of the blood must be done with the utmost care, as it can become separated and lose its strength. A very important factor to be considered before giving human blood to others is that the blood types must match. As a former blood donor, it is very humbling and rewarding to know that my pints of blood could have possibly helped others to live.

Yes, our blood has the potential to save a few lives, but it is nothing compared to Jesus's blood. Without exception, his blood can save all. Just what makes the blood of Jesus so different? What makes his blood so powerful that it transcends time and blood types, never loses its strength, and remains effective for all eternity?

As we look at history, the first Adam had no mother. Therefore, the blood that ran through Adam's veins could only come from his parent: God. At the time of Adam's creation, he received untainted, pure blood. This blood remained pure and undefiled up to the moment he sinned. After the fall of man, the blood became corrupted, and Adam passed it down to all human beings except Jesus. When God got ready to redeem human beings, he sent his seed filled with his divine blood to impregnate the Virgin Mary. He was making it possible to rid us of the sin-filled, corrupted blood that had been in the world since the fall of man. The blood of Jesus withstood the distance of travel from heaven to earth and back to heaven without losing any of its strength.

Unlike human blood, his blood has a nonexpiring shelf life, for it still covers you and me and all who will come after us; it is a forever sacrifice. Jesus shed his blood and died once and for all—one time.

> Much more then, having now been justified by His blood, we shall be saved from wrath through Him. (Romans 5:9 NKJV)

> Therefore, as through one man's offense judgment came to all men, resulting in condemnation, even

> so through one Man's righteous act the free gift
> came to all men, resulting in justification of life.
> (Romans 5:18 NKJV)

Through the offense of Adam, we were born guilty and condemned to a hopeless future; the result of that person is death and total separation from God. Being justified by God is not automatic; it must be applied to your life. All of us are born condemned. Therefore, each of us must choose to be justified by a holy and righteous God. We do not cross over into justification with the age of accountability. With the age of accountability comes a responsibility by the person to choose the righteous act of Jesus that makes you a new creature in Christ.

Justification is God choosing the punishment for the crime (sin) and then nailing his only begotten Son to the cross to pay for it. Jesus died so that sinful man might be made right in God's sight. Yes, we were guilty; we deserved to die and to be banished to hell. Romans 6:23 (NIV) says, "For the wages of sin is death, but the gift of God is eternal life in Christ Jesus our Lord." Our sin nailed Jesus to that cross. But justification says, "The debt has been satisfied; no further payment is necessary."

As we walk in the newness of life given to us by God, our former life is no longer visible to him, for when God looks at the new creation, he now sees the righteousness of his Son, Jesus. Righteousness is the result of justification in that God chose to punish his Son, Jesus, to die in order that sinful man might be made right. Now there is nothing holding us back from knowing God, except ourselves. Not only are we free, but also we have been given twenty-four-seven access to communicate with the Father, just like Jesus had when he lived on earth. It is the new state of being for the believer in Christ, and it is that person's new nature.

> No one who is born of God will continue to sin, because God's seed remains in them; they cannot go on sinning, because they have been born of God. (1 John 3:9 NIV)

Righteousness is God breathing a fresh beginning on you. It says now you are free from the guilt that once covered you in sin. Would a person who was on trial and found not guilty be required to come back to court for the verdict to be read repeatedly? Of course not, for there would be no need for him to appear before the judge on that charge again. Everyone involved understands the law; this person is now free to go on with his life. Because you and I are born of God, we have been made righteous. Therefore, we must readily accept God's verdict that we have been cleared of all wrongdoing.

> That you may be children of your Father in heaven. He causes his sun to rise on the evil and the good, and sends rain on the righteous and the unrighteous. (Matthew 5:45 NIV)

From the scripture above, we see a loving God who is impartial to providing for the needs of all humankind. The substance he provides, such as food, shelter, and clothing, only pertain to man's physical life here on earth. Jehovah-Sabaoth (Lord of hosts) is the creator of the earth, and he knows how to be a good host while maintaining his standards. God has drawn a line in the sand and has left it up to us to choose a side. One side is for the righteous (those who have been justified), and the other side is for the unrighteous (those still guilty). We tend to think that there is no distinction between those in Christ and those outside of Christ because of our outward appearance. We live in the same type of houses, shop at the same stores, go to school together, and work with each other; the similarities in our lives are numerous.

By viewing all human lives on the surface, we cannot understand all the benefits that God has given us as believers. As residents of the earth, the righteous and unrighteous have an entitlement to the same provisions. However, for the righteous in Christ, the benefits go beyond our basic needs. God has provided us with his Holy Spirit; we have divine health, his peace, his authority, power, and favor.

Another benefit that is uniquely for the righteous in Christ is prayer. God welcomes the righteous man or woman at all times. Those who are unrighteous have no legal grounds to come before him in prayer. John 9:31 (NKJV) says, "Now we know that God does not hear sinners; but if anyone is a worshipper of God and does His will, He hears him." This scripture is as clear-cut as it gets, in that it is founded on the principle that God never wavers in his standards of whom he considers righteous. As a believer in Christ, you have been made righteous in his sight and have unlimited access to come before him in prayer. To the person who has not given his or her life over to the Lord, God has purposely blocked the pathway between that person and himself.

Lamentations 3:44 says, "You have covered Yourself with a cloud; that prayer should not pass through" (NKJV).

If people have not made Jesus Lord of their life, God is angry with them. Psalm 7:11 (NKJV) says, "God is a just judge, And God is angry with the wicked every day." To this day for the unrighteous, God's standard remains in place; there will be no communication between the unrighteous person and God, unless the person repents and accepts Jesus as Lord. We see here that a clear pathway to God is only for the righteous. Because we have been exonerated by the blood of Christ, the cloud that prevented our prayers from getting through to God has been taken away. The blood of Jesus now ties you and me directly to God, with nothing in between us. Now you are free to come to him and make your request known.

Being righteous is not you or me trying to keep the law and the Ten Commandments. We cannot in ourselves earn righteousness by being good. No matter how hard we try to do right in this life, it does not qualify us as righteous. This righteousness that God has bestowed upon us happened for one reason only: we have received his Son as our Savior.

None of our good works will ever be good enough to be called righteous. No amount of money you give to a charity or time you donate to a worthy cause will make you righteous in God's sight. As believers in Christ, we must honor God's word by accepting the truth that the blood of Christ alone has made us righteous in his sight. As long as we are in our bodies, the ability to sin will always be with us. Therefore, we must choose to walk in the righteousness that was given to us when we became born again.

The umbilical cord connects the baby to the mother while in the womb. The umbilical cord along with the placenta takes the place of the baby's lungs. However, once the baby is born into the world, he or she begins to breathe on his or her own. As born-again believers, our old sin nature is replaced with our new nature: righteousness. As we know, a baby born cannot return to the mother's womb. But God gives us a choice: we can remain in our old sin nature and eventually die, or we can embrace our new nature of righteousness and have eternal life. The latter is the way God intends for us to live on earth.

> For He made Him who knew no sin to be sin for us, that we might become the righteousness of God in Him. (2 Corinthians 5:21NKJV)

After the fall, Adam was naked and ashamed and desperately wanted to cover up. His once-perfect world, where righteousness was the rule, was suddenly gone. Adam had a bigger problem than being physically naked, for the spirit within him was now dead. God clothed Adam and Eve with clothes made of animal skin by performing the first sacrifice. This sacrifice would be the first of many to come. The act of covering the outward man with clothes could not fix the real problem. It was a temporary solution for humans until God's plan could be fulfilled.

Like Adam before the fall, all of us are born into this world physically naked. Since the fall of man, we are all born (except Jesus) into unrighteousness. Though our outward man at birth is immediately clothed, our inward man is not. Then along comes Jesus, the ultimate sacrifice. He shed his blood so that you and

I might choose to be clothed in righteousness. Our once-dead spirits have now been made alive.

The icing on the cake for a movie actor is an Oscar or a Tony award if you are on Broadway. For stars on television, their big moment of recognition comes with an Emmy. Music stars winning a Grammy or a Dove award for their musical contributions is the highlight of their career. One of the highest honors an individual can achieve in the United Kingdom is that of knighthood (male) or damehood (female). This honor is bestowed by the monarch to individuals who have made a significant contribution to national life. When the monarch of England knights someone, that person is given a new title, sir for males and dame for women. There are many prestigious awards given all over the world to individuals someone deems worthy. Some of us, including myself, have been the recipient of such an award. Now, for the man or woman who have been made the righteousness of Christ, there are no first place and second place winners. For all are winners. My righteousness in Christ is the same as your righteousness in Christ. The difference between the world's accolades and God's accolades is that the world rewards the best of the best here and now. God rewards us with the crown of righteousness in heaven for all eternity, for the way we lived here on earth.

The righteousness of Christ in the believer comes with a spiritual viewpoint of life on earth. For me, things that I once had no conviction about became clear that they were offensive to God. For instance, before salvation, I thought nothing of watching an X-rated (pornographic) movie or telling "little white lies" like calling into work and saying I was sick when I was not sick. The righteousness of Christ came upon us to produce good fruit. Therefore, we are encouraged by the Holy Spirit to put away all lies and uncleanness and anything that does not bring glory to God. Because we are the righteousness of Christ, you and I must make better choices on the things we will allow in our lives. Our standard of living has been upgraded high above all other human beings living on the earth.

> This is the confidence we have in approaching God: that if we ask anything according to his will, he hears us. And if we know that he hears us— whatever we ask—we know that we have what we asked of him. (1 John 5:14–15 NIV)

The devil, who is the master of deception, will try to tell you that this does not apply to you. He is always on the prowl, seeking to tamper with our understanding that we are in right standing with God. The only people who are guilty are the ones who have not accepted Jesus's sacrifice on the cross. If the devil can get us to vacillate between knowing we are accepted and forgiven by God versus we are not quite right with God, we will hesitate to come boldly before God's throne. If we keep before us the image of our accepting Jesus as Lord of our lives, we are now free to live as those who have been accepted and approved by God. Having received the heavenly blood of Jesus is proof of my exoneration. It is God's desire and will for our lives that we no longer approach him timidly or with doubt, but that we recognize that we have a right as believers in Christ to come before him.

Let us then approach God's throne of grace with confidence, so that we may receive mercy and find grace to help us in our time of need. (Hebrew 4:16 NIV)

Chapter 2

Reconciled

There is a way that appears to be right, but in the
end, it leads to death. (Proverbs 14:12 NIV)

Mistakes happen all the time, right? I wrote a children's book
a few years ago titled, *The Adventures of Sam and Clue*. Despite
proofreading by myself and several others, the first edition of
the book contained a word error. The word *where* should have
been *were* in one of the sentences. The mistake was corrected
at once by the publisher, but nevertheless, the first edition had
gone out with the error, for everyone reading the book to see.
Was this embarrassing for me? Of course it was. But there have
been mistakes made, with far costlier consequences than that of
the integrity of a book. A prime example is the sinking of the
Titanic back in April of 1912. Regardless of how it happened,
many lives were lost needlessly as a result of the mistakes that
were made during that fatal voyage. Human error has resulted
in numerous chemical plant explosions, nuclear plant explosions,
and even some oil spills, which has resulted in the loss of human

and animal lives. As with the error in my book, some mistakes can easily be corrected. But then there are other mistakes made that will have a lasting effect on people's lives.

> When the woman saw that the fruit of the tree was good for food and pleasing to the eye, and also desirable for gaining wisdom, she took some and ate it. She also gave some to her husband, who was with her, and he ate it. (Genesis 3:6 NIV)

Many mistakes have been made throughout history. Still, there has never been nor ever will be a mistake as costly as the one made by the first man—Adam. When Adam ate the fruit from the tree of the knowledge of good and evil, he started a down-trodden movement for humankind that only God could rectify. After Adam sinned, his spirit within him died; the part of him that was created to live forever was gone in a flash. It was Adam the spirit man, who walked with God in the cool of the day. Life as he knew it would never be the same. Since that colossal of a mistake occurred, the human race now had a big problem. They were forced to live life as enemies of God (Romans 5:10). Man's downgraded life would be full of sorrow, burdensome labor, immense pain, and an uncertainty of the future. This new life for Adam and Eve was quite the contrast from the life they lived in the garden of Eden.

Can you image how perfect life was for Adam and Eve before the fall? Everything was always good because good was all they knew. For Adam and Eve, evil did not exist. They had complete dominion over everything that moved in the earth. It was heaven indeed on earth for the first couple. Adam and Eve never knew friction between each other. No one ever went to bed angry. There was no need for a doctor, for in Adam and Eve's perfect world they were never sick. Most importantly of all, they could communicate with God every day, for there was never anything to distract them from being in his presence.

Yes, life was excellent for the original first couple, and all that was required of them by the Lord was to obey him. But of course, there was an enemy in the camp, and unbeknownst to Adam and Eve, Satan's intentions were to destroy them, and it worked. However, unknown to the enemy, God had a plan to reconcile man back to himself. From the moment of the fall, the plan was set in motion by God to redeem humans back to himself, but it would take a few thousand years for it to manifest.

God had to remove the man from the garden for his own good because the tree of life was in the garden of Eden (Genesis 3:23–24). If man took and ate from it, he would live forever. No flesh was designed to live forever without the spirit. God took Adam out of his comfort zone and forced him to toil and labor for the rest of his life. The fruit of sin soon manifested with Adam's firstborn son, Cain. Cain, as a result of sin, was angry at God and was jealous because his brother Abel offered an acceptable sacrifice to God. Now, being unwilling to accept God's good advice (Genesis 4:7), Cain chose to follow evil and murdered his brother. So we see the sin of Adam fell on his son, and it is still falling to this day on the sons and daughters of Adam.

Just as one man's sinful act broke holy fellowship with God, one man's righteous act has the power to restore holy fellowship back to God. God's plan was revealed with the birth of his Son Jesus. Reconciliation between God and man occurred with the death of Jesus on the cross. With the resurrection of Christ came the opportunity of a lifetime. By accepting Jesus as your personal Savior, you are in a win-win situation. You get to have a great life here on earth, and an even greater life (eternal) when you get to heaven. Reconciliation to God has now made it possible for us to choose good and shun evil. Yes, evil is always lurking around us, but the goodness of God is consistently following us.

> Brethren, do not be children in understanding; however in malice be babes, but in understanding be mature. (1 Corinthians 14:20 NKJV)

As a little girl, I rarely got in trouble with my parents, but there were times I needed correcting. During those times, I would stay mad at my parents for weeks. I just could not bring myself to talk to them. I had no problem with my parents providing for my needs—food, clothing, and shelter—but communicating with them was a different story. I would only respond to their questions with an indifferent yes or no. Before we got saved, we treated God in this same manner. Still, there are some of us treating him in the same way after salvation. We will take what we need from him but have little to no communication with him or respect for him. This lack of communication with him and respect to God is the result of us not knowing that once we have been justified and made righteous, we have no valid reason to treat God in this manner. I treated my parents unfairly out of ignorance of not understanding that I was to honor them at all times. Now, if you are treating God in this manner that to results from a lack of understanding.

> Once you were alienated from God and were enemies in your minds because of your evil behavior. But now he has reconciled you by Christ's physical body through death to present you holy in his sight, without blemish and free from accusation. (Colossians 1:21–22 NIV)

Looking back, I recall the reason I would hold a grudge against my mom or dad was that I wanted them to feel bad for punishing me. In my mind, the cold shoulder was the best way to accomplish my mission. I held on to that behavior after I got married, and I began to treat my husband the same way. Once I became reconciled to God, my evil behavior toward my loved ones was turned around for the good. Reconciled means to be brought back into right standing with God, no longer an enemy, no more enmity, revived from spiritual death. God has reconciled us back to himself by restoring the spirit man within us.

One day at work I was talking with one of my coworkers. I was sharing an experience I recently had and mentioned being a born-again Christian. With a puzzled expression on her face, she asked me what a born-again Christian was. My coworker grew up in the church but had never known what it meant to be born again. She had assumed this was a particular denomination term, and therefore, it did not apply to her. I began to share with my coworker the meaning of John 3:1–8. After you have accepted Jesus as your Savior, you are born for the second time. This time, however, it is your spirit (the real you) that has been made alive. We can be assured that if it is in the Bible, it is for all those who have accepted Jesus as Lord of their lives. The only way a person can be reconciled to God is by having a born-again experience with the Holy Spirit.

> Now it is God who makes both us and you stand firm in Christ. He anointed us, set his seal of ownership on us, and put his Spirit in our hearts as a deposit, guaranteeing what is to come. (2 Corinthians 1:21–22 NIV)

In the United States, there is a Bipartisan Campaign Reform Act, which requires a political candidate for a federal office to make a statement at the end of the television or radio ad to identify his or her approval of the message. They usually give their name and then say, "I approve this message." With this Reform Act in place, candidates are less likely to fund attack ads against their opponents. When we give our hearts to God, and he reconciles us back to himself, he sends a message to the spiritual world identifying you and me as belonging to him. God is saying to all, "I am the Lord, and I approve of this man or woman." Psalm 103:11–12 (NIV) says, "For as high as the heavens are above the earth, so great is his love for those who fear him; as far as the east is from the west, so far has he removed our transgressions from us." Reconciliation to God means we have been forgiven for the sin passed down to us from the first man, Adam. Your record has been cleared up by the Lord, and he no longer counts your sin against you. Now, all the privileges that belong to Jesus have instantly become ours at our new birth. One of the privileges given to us is God's full protection from the enemy forever. John 10:29 (NIV) says, "My Father, who has given them to me, is greater than all; no one can snatch them out of my Father's hand." From the moment we accepted Jesus as our personal Savior, the Holy Spirit was sent to live in our hearts. The Holy Spirit is our guarantee from God that we have eternal life. It is the Holy Spirit who will one day escort us into the very presence of God.

> For He rescued us from the domain of darkness,
> and transferred us to the kingdom of His beloved
> Son, in whom we have redemption, the forgiveness
> of sins. (Colossians 1:13–14 NIV)

Chapter 3

Spiritually Alive

Therefore, if anyone is in Christ, he is a new creation; old things have passed away; behold, all things have become new. (2 Corinthians 5:17 NKJV)

It's big! It is the biggest news we could ever receive. We no longer have to exist in this lost and dying world as mere human beings. I know it sounds crazy. We have been referring to ourselves as human beings all our lives. God wants us to understand how critical it is to know that we are spiritually alive. Yes, we have all heard it, and many of us quote it: "I am a spirit, I have a mind, and I live in a body." For most of us, that is what it amounts to—just a quote. Without a true understanding of what it means to be alive in Christ, we will keep right on living life as usual. We will still walk in conditional love toward others; we will serve God out of our own strength or make rash decisions based on our feelings of the moment. As a result of not understanding our new nature, we could slip into eternity one day, not knowing that there was so much more that God had for us. All of this is about to change because we now understand justification, which makes us the righteousness of Christ, and we have been reconciled to God.

It does not matter whether you have been saved five minutes, five years, or fifty years—waking up with a renewed understanding of being a spiritual being is pretty awesome. Your whole perception about living this life on earth will change when you realize that a new life has begun in you. One of the first changes I noticed about myself was I became more aware of other people. There was one lady at a church I once attended who was physically blind but always appeared to have enormous peace and joy every Sunday. I used to wonder how that was possible since she always had to depend on others. Soon afterward, I discovered that joy does not come from your outward condition, good or bad. I found out that being spiritually alive includes having the peace that surpasses all understanding and that joy comes from the Lord. What a contrast from the people of the world, who need things and right conditions to experience a temporary happiness. But we who are alive in Christ have an automatic fountain of joy in our inner being, and that fountain will never run dry.

> For Christ also suffered once for sins, the just for the unjust, that He might bring us to God, being put to death in the flesh but made alive by the Spirit. (1 Peter 3:18 NKJV)

God used my love for reading to draw me to Jesus. Growing up, I had very little experience with going to church. I did go to my grandmother's church for about a year, but I still did not know God. I became an avid reader of romance novels beginning with my teenage years. This love affair with reading continued after I was married. One day home alone, I was without a fresh book to read, so I grabbed the dusty Bible off of the bookcase. I began reading the Bible from the beginning as if were a novel. A couple of months later while reading in the book of Romans, for the first time in my life, I knew I needed Jesus. I can recall the exact moment in time when I received Jesus as my Savior and was renewed in my inner being. I was home in my bedroom, sitting on the floor when the love of God drew me to repentance of my present way of life. Afterward, even though I had changed, I still did not grasp the meaning of being made spiritually alive in my relationship with God. I knew that something big had happened to me and that I was changed from the inside out, but I still lacked understanding of being alive in Christ and dead to this world. Yes, I was a new creature in Christ, but it did not stop the wars from going on inside of me. I still struggled with my identity as a believer in Christ. I was not able to comprehend what my new status as a believer meant. I knew I was saved and on my way to heaven (one day), but I did not understand that I was to live as a spiritual being in Christ every day and all day.

Whether we grasped the meaning of being spiritually alive goes back to the very foundation of not what we have received from God but rather how we perceived it. It was my understanding that being saved meant I was now to be a better person. If we do not grasp the process of being made spiritually alive, then we go through this life circling the mountain of misunderstanding. We have been born again as spiritual beings while we still live in our earthly (human) bodies. God loves us so much that he has taken the time to teach us in his word what it means to be spiritually alive and how to remain in this wonderful condition. To be spiritually alive is you waking up from being dead inside and knowing that you have been made alive in Christ.

> Now when He was asked by the Pharisees when the kingdom of God would come, He answered them and said, "The kingdom of God does not come with observation; nor will they say, 'See here!' or 'See there!' For indeed, the kingdom of God is within you." (Luke 17:20–21 NKJV)

We must reverse the order by which we live our daily lives. Our task is to embrace our spirituality while adjusting to the human nature in us as being secondary in our lives. We must become true to our new life in Christ. We are created to live a supernatural life as Jesus lived when he walked the earth. When Jesus lived on earth, everything about him wanted to please God. Our inheritance on earth is that we can become God pleasers by living a supernatural life. We start the process of living this life on earth by first identifying with the Holy Spirit of God who happens to live in our spirit. A supernatural life is based on living in the kingdom of God rather than living according to the rudiments and traditions, or the latest technology in this world.

In the kingdom of God, there is absolute loyalty to the one who sits on the throne. What God says goes, and there is never any room for discussion in his kingdom. It is not a democracy. There are no surprises in his kingdom. You know exactly where he stands on everything about living on earth. God has no hidden agendas. It is a requirement that all who live in his kingdom, view life from his perspective. If there is something we struggle to come to terms with, God is willing to help us overcome that area. However, the result must be that we side with the Lord. All we have to do is walk in obedience and carry out his commandments. The safest place for a believer in Christ is in the perfect will of the Lord. As we take on our new position in God's kingdom, we become like the angels in heaven, who have no agendas of their own. They simply do what God tells them to do because they exist to please him.

It was for his pleasure the angels were created, and it is for his pleasure we the children of God are created. Revelation 4:11 (NIV) says, "You are worthy, our Lord and God, to receive glory and honor and power, for you created all things, and by your will they were created and have their being." As created beings, we do not have the right to take upon ourselves the authority to govern our lives. God in his infinite wisdom decided long ago the best course for each of our lives. If we are to exist in his kingdom, we must first dethrone ourselves off of our own hearts. There is never any room for more than one king in every believer's heart. You must choose your position here on earth. Either you are a subject in his kingdom, or you are a slave to this world and everything it stands for. Your actions will always give you away as to where your heart lies.

> I have been crucified with Christ, and I no longer
> live, but Christ lives in me. The life I now live

in the body, I live by faith in the Son of God,
who loved me and gave himself for me. (Galatians
2:20 NIV)

It is impossible for us to be alive in Christ and alive to the
world at the same time. God did not send his Son into the world
so you and I could live life straddling the fence. It comes down to
you and me understanding that we cannot be alive to both Christ
and the world. We must stop wavering and make a decision. Do I
go ahead and accept my status as a spiritually alive person, or do
I keep hoping that when I stand before God, my good works will
outweigh my bad actions? Paul makes it very clear in this scripture
that after we are born again, we only live because of Christ.

When my husband and I got married, my last name was
legally changed from Lucas to Davis. To this day, no matter what
is going on in my marriage, my last name is Davis. I do not get
to change it back to Lucas based on my feelings. I am bound in
the eyes of God to my husband and to wearing his last name
until death do we part. It is the duty of every believer in Christ
to change his or her perspective on how we should live here on
earth. I ceased being Betty Lucas the moment I said I do, and
the minister pronounced us man and wife. We cease to be just an
ordinary citizen of this world the moment we accepted Jesus into
our lives. Now, we belong to him and must live solely for him.
Just as Jesus walked the earth as a spiritual being in a human
being's body, we are to do the same. We are bound in the eyes of
God to live for Christ. Our old life is dead, and our new life in
Christ has begun.

Do not love the world or anything in the world. If anyone loves the world, love for the Father is not in them. (1 John 2:15 NIV)

To live for Jesus means we have to become as he was on earth. To become imitators of Jesus, we must love what he loves, hate what he hates, and live in this world as he did. Jesus did not love this world or the things of this world. He came to save humanity from a life destined to eternal damnation. Jesus's focus was always his Father and the work he sent him to earth to do. Jesus was so in love with his Father and the life he had previously lived in heaven, that when he finished his work on earth, he said to his Father, "And now, O Father, glorify Me together with Yourself, with the glory which I had with You before the world was" (John 17:5 NKJV). Jesus was ready to go back home to heaven, so he left us well equipped to continue his work on earth by making us spiritually alive. And to be spiritually alive is to accept the responsibility for the work of Christ on the earth. Jesus passed the baton to the new creatures in the earth, and he ordered you and me to go and make disciples of others (Matthew 28:18–20).

Chapter 4

Deliberately Left Behind

My prayer is not that you take them out of the
world but that you protect them from the evil one.
(John 17:15 NIV)

Left Behind, by Tim LaHaye and Jerry B. Jenkins, is one of my
all-time favorite book series. In fact, I read most of the books
in the series twice. I even read the *Left Behind* kids' series as
well. Reading the book series caused excitement in me, knowing
that the rapture of the believers could take place in my lifetime.
During that period, I had a coworker named Mike who was not
a believer in Christ, yet he respected my position as a Christian.
Mike never went out of his way to avoid talking to me, as others
would. He generally would be the one to initiate the conversation
about Jesus and the things of God. I used to tell Mike that if the
rapture were to happen, that he was to break into my house and
take the *Left Behind* books. I deliberately placed those books in a
place where he could easily find them. I also kept a Bible on my
desk at work, and in the case of my disappearance, I told him he

should take it as well. With the *Left Behind* books and the Bible, I believed Mike would become a tribulation believer and would in turn rescue others doomed for destruction.

Just as I was setting my coworker up to take my place on earth, Jesus in his infinite wisdom set us up as his successors to rescue others in this world. Jesus requested to the Father that you and I be left here on earth. Our mission is found in Matthew 28:19 (NIV): "Therefore go and make disciples of all nations, baptizing them in the name of the Father and of the Son and of the Holy Spirit." He never intended to set up his kingdom here on earth but to make it possible for workers (that is you and me) to continue the work he had begun. Acts 17:28 (NIV) says, "For in him we live and move and have our being. As some of your own poets have said, 'We are his offspring.'" As an offspring of God, nothing is too difficult or impossible for you to overcome as you carry out the work he left you here to do.

Jesus did not leave us in this world unprotected. No, he made sure the Father would provide the security we needed to be safe from the evil one. God did this by sending to us the only one who could be with us always. The Holy Spirit was introduced to us at the moment we were saved. He came bearing gifts, giving us what we could not have apart from him. God never intended for the Holy Spirit to be a part of this world; he was only to live in us as we live in the world. The Holy Spirit is here to teach us how to live life as spiritual beings in human bodies. When you follow the lead of the Holy Spirit, he will lead you away from the traps of the enemy every time. The Holy Spirit of God knows his job through and through. He is here for the long haul to see that you and I carry out the work the Lord left for us to do. (Further teaching on the Holy Spirit can be found in chapter 7, "Led by the Spirit.")

As new creatures in Christ, a correct understanding of *in the world* versus *of the world* is necessary. As long as you are in the world only, you are under God's protection. When you live your life as of this world, then you remove yourself from God's full protection. For then, there is no guarantee of your safety. When you are of this world, you cannot do the work the Lord left you here to do. You are an open target for the enemy. It is critical for us as born-again believers in Christ to understand the difference between in and of.

In—used to indicate location or position within something. It merely tells where I am physically placed at this time. In the case of the world, you do not feel as if you belong to it because you have been born again.

Of—belonging to, relating to, or connected with (someone or something). Of is when I am mentally as well as physically connected to this place I am currently in. I feel a sense of belonging to it.

I retired after thirty-five years as a state employee. Throughout the years, I developed a daily routine. The first thing I would do when I got home from work was to change into more comfortable clothing. And I always changed my shoes and put on my house slippers. I took great pleasure in doing this, as it signified to me that I was home, with my family. Now, if I were to go to your house, I would not expect to be as comfortable in your house, simply because it is not mine. That is how it is meant to be; I would just be visiting you, with no intention of living with you.

When Jesus was here on earth, he reminded his disciples that this world was not his home. Jesus had a job to do on earth, and nothing was going to stop him from accomplishing his mission. Therefore, I am sure he never mentally took off of his shoes to put on some house slippers. Rather, Jesus keep his work shoes on. The more I understand about being in this world (to work) and not of this world (to stay), I am beginning to keep my work shoes mentally on.

> Now then, we are ambassadors for Christ, as though God were pleading through us: we implore you on Christ's behalf, be reconciled to God. (2 Corinthians 5:20 NKJV)

Our mission on earth is to understand what the will of God is for our lives. God has uniquely given to each of us an assignment, yet corporately it is the same result—to go and make disciples. Jesus's desire is that we pull out as many as we can from this world. Our job is to take others out of this world by patterning our lives after Jesus's when he was on earth. Jesus never compromised with this world, for the world was his mission field. My local church supports missionaries. One of our missionary couples recently adopted a child from Africa. As Americans, it was important for their son to be an American citizen as well. Africa is a place where they were called to work, with the understanding that they would eventually go back home to America. They did not give up their rights as US citizens but merely were answering a call from God, to go to a foreign land. As it is with most missionaries, the goal is to leave home, get the job done, and go back home.

How Jesus looked forward to going home to his Father, surrounded by the heavenly host. His seat was waiting there for him, right beside the Father at his right hand. Jesus is at this moment, preparing a place for you and me. He left us here in the world, to continue God's work.

> Now I am no longer in the world, but these are in the world, and I come to You. Holy Father, keep through Your name those whom You have given Me that they may be one as We are. (John 17:11 NKJV)

It is interesting that Jesus in John 17:11 said, "Now I am no longer in the world ..." He was physically living, breathing, and speaking to God at that time. And we know that his death on the cross had not occurred. But clearly, Jesus had already checked out and was on his way to heaven to be with his Father. Jesus was speaking as one who was not here on earth. When Jesus was on earth, he was constantly talking to the Father. When elementary kids are in school, most states have a mandatory requirement of recess for the students. The first thing most kids want to do is go outside and play with others. As adults, we too need down time, away from our jobs. When Jesus took a break from working, he preferred going to a solitary place to pray to his Father. That was how Jesus preferred spending his recess. As an adult, how do you prefer to spend your recess?

As long as it is day, we must do the works of him
who sent me. Night is coming, when no one can
work. While I am in the world, I am the light of
the world. (John 9:4–5 NIV)

As we open our eyes to the truth, we will see Jesus as he
illuminates the work fields of the world, by showing us the sin-
filled lives of men and women who are perishing. For without
Jesus as Lord of your life, your world is without Son light. We
can see the fields and the harvest because of the supernatural light
shining on them. People living without Jesus as their light will
continue to sit in darkness while going about their day-to-day
activities. People who have not received Jesus as Lord are blind
and cannot see the truth—that without Christ no man is living
as God would have them to live. God's purpose for shining Jesus
as the light of the world is so that we who belong to Christ will
not work in darkness.

While Jesus is no longer physically in the world, he is still
in the world through you and me. With Jesus as the light of the
world, God has provided everything we need to complete the
work in his field. Every time Jesus spoke of the world in John
17, as it applies to himself or the believers, he referred to it as we
being in the world. He makes it quite clear that we who belong to
him are not of this world. We are only here on a temporary visa
to work in it. Night is coming, and life as we know it will come
to an end for each of us one day, and we will no longer be able
to work. With that in mind, how should you and I be spending
our recesses?

Chapter 5

The Abundance of Life

> Why, you do not even know what will happen
> tomorrow. What is your life? You are a mist that
> appears for a little while and then vanishes. (James
> 4:14 NIV)

A mist. A vapor. A puff of smoke. Steam coming from the cooking
pot on the stove. Our life is but a mist, like the fragrance from a
squirt of perfume, that is soon to disappear. Compared to eternity,
that is what our lives look like on earth, something that is virtually
here today and gone tomorrow. Generation after generation, they
all end the same way. One after another, we all die out. Is this
what all the fuss is about? In John 10:10 (NKJV) it says, "The
thief does not come except to steal, and to kill, and to destroy."
Is this what the thief is really after in us, our brief existence on
earth as human beings? Do you think the thief cares about your
financial state of being, whether you are rich or poor? In the same
scripture, Jesus says, "I have come that they may have life, and that
they may have it more abundantly." Did Jesus sacrifice himself

on the cross for the brief time we will spend on earth? Or is he referring to a life deeper than the physical life?

As we stop and think about it, only the living (those breathing) can get saved and become born again. So the physical life is not the life Jesus came to give us because all living human beings possess a physical life. And if he did not come to give us something we already have, it stands to reason that *abundantly* has very little to do with the things we use in this world. There are many people in this world who are rich and have all the things that money can buy. Yet, these same people are lost because they have not accepted the life that Jesus came to give them.

> And when Jesus had cried out again in a loud voice, he gave up his spirit. At that moment the curtain of the temple was torn in two from top to bottom. The earth shook, the rocks split. (Matthew 27:50–51 NIV)

Mission accomplished! The plan to redeem man back to his original state of being has been set in motion. Access to a completely spiritual being was given to the believer at the moment of salvation. God made it possible for us to live on earth as his Son did while he was here. When Jesus walked the earth, he was all spirit in a body. The fact that he had bodily needs like eating, sleeping, drinking, etc., did not take away from him being all spirit. As new creatures, we too are spiritual beings, but just having our basic needs as humans fulfilled is not enough for us. Unlike Jesus, our wants and desires are often centered around the material things of this world. Therefore, the things that are beyond our basic needs that we receive from God become our blessings and our perception of abundance of life.

We generally want more and bigger and better. It is a dream we been carrying with us throughout this life. As human beings, it is in our nature to live or desire to live a financially prosperous life. But if the funds began to dry up, or it never materializes in our life, do we ever consider that perhaps God had something to do with it? The Bible says in Ecclesiastes 7:13–14 (NKJV) that God has appointed prosperity as well as adversity. A prime example is Job, a man who lived a godly life, who was prosperous, and yet he lost it all. The thief (Satan) was the mastermind behind the attack. Satan was given permission by God to do whatever he wanted to do to Job's possessions. Not only was Job a godly man, but he was a smart man as well, for he recognized that everything he had was given to him by the Lord and that it was the Lord who took it away. In spite of it all, Job still blessed the name of the Lord (Job 1:21). Job's abundant life was not found in his possessions. Abundant life for Job was in his relationship with God.

What more can be said about this abundant life we have been given? We all have heard the rumor mill as believers that abundant life is Jesus coming that we might have more materially speaking than we had before. And how about the one where God wants us to have money so we can show the world that we are the most blessed people on earth? As believers, we have brought into the misnomer that everything we get materially is a blessing, even if we borrowed to get it. And even then, man decides when it is to be considered a blessing, such as financing a house, a vehicle, or an education. Yes, we are told that taking out a student loan for a college education is an acceptable thing to do because it could mean a higher salary for you when you start your career. But all these things are done by nonbelievers as well. Therefore, there is nothing special about the abundant material life. When we equate having material possessions with abundant living, we are putting the Lord of all in a small box. God does not mimic the world; everything he does is an original work. God has charted the course for every believer's life on earth, and no two paths are the same.

It is time that we rethink our viewpoint about abundant living and align ourselves with Jesus when he walked the earth. As we study the life of Jesus, we find nowhere in the gospels where he focused on making a living, having a career, having a retirement plan, or investing for the future. No, he was about spending his "mist" of his physical life doing the will of his Father and investing in the lives of others. We tend to spend more time making sure our financial house is in order than we do our spiritual house, which is the real us. There is a thin line between the world's view of finances and a Christian's view on finances. Financial advisors, whether they are Christians or not, are saying the same thing: earn, budget, save, and even give. Yes, the people of the world give to charities too. The main difference is that Christians are taught to tithe 10 percent to God.

Let's face it—all money looks the same, be it the money of the righteous or the unrighteous. More importantly, all money spends the same. What is it that sets the believers apart from the world when it comes to finances? There must be something that can distinguish us from those who are in the world. How did

Jesus handle finances? When Jesus was confronted about his debt (taxes owed to the government), what did he do? Did he panic and begin to worry? Did he run out and tried to find a job right quick? No, he used a very unorthodox method to attain the necessary monies. Jesus sent Peter fishing, to catch a fish he had waiting for him with money in its mouth. In Matthew 17:24–27 this passage gives us a clear view of God's viewpoint that our ways are not his ways. How many of us would have thought of getting money out of a fish mouth to pay our taxes? Not only was there enough money to pay Jesus's taxes, but Peter's taxes as well. Could you get use to God taking care of your earthly needs in that manner? I certainly could.

There are testimonies from people all over the world of God supernaturally providing for someone's needs—testimonies such as receiving unexpected checks in the mail with the exact amount needed by the recipient or someone going to pay a bill only to be told by the creditor that it has already been paid. When we limit God to the conventional ways of buying, selling, and paying bills, you are literally saying this is my comfort level in receiving from God. Ephesians 3:20 (NKJV) says, "Now to Him who is able to do exceedingly abundantly above all that we ask or think, according to the power that works in us." God is not limited to your paycheck in providing for your needs. He has resources you and I could not imagine. As we began to shift our thinking from the traditional viewpoints of finances to God's viewpoint, we will see as his word says in Luke 1:37 (NKJV), "For with God nothing will be impossible."

If abundant life is not about your financial status here on

earth, what is it about? Abundant life is about your spiritual state of being and your relationship with God. It is your understanding of who you are in Christ and the position he has given you in the earth. For out of this knowledge comes everything you need on earth to be pleasing to God. Everything we get or have on earth is considered lagniappe. Lagniappe means something given as a bonus or extra gift. Your beautiful home, fine cars, and expensive jewelry are just lagniappe for you to enjoy while you live here on earth. Abundance to the believer in Christ is everything you get to take back to heaven with you.

> Do not lay up for yourselves treasures on earth, where moth and rust destroy and where thieves break in and steal; but lay up for yourselves treasures in heaven, where neither moth nor rust destroys and where thieves do not break in and steal. (Matthew 6:19–20 NKJV)

When God, Jesus, the Holy Spirit, and the angels see those who have become new creatures in Christ, they do not see our flesh. As new creatures in Christ, we have been adopted into the family of God as spiritual beings in human bodies. But because our flesh is ever present with us, and with a little help from the world, we continue to see ourselves in the physical world as fleshly beings. The enemy is counting on us to hold on to this way of thinking. If we stay busy, living life as ordinary human beings, we are less likely to focus on the spiritual aspect of our lives. When humanity in us gets the bulk of our time and attention, it is impossible to live our lives based on the new nature we have received. The biggest threat to the enemy in your life is when you discover your hidden life in Christ.

> No weapon formed against you shall prosper, and every tongue which rises against you in judgment You shall condemn. This is the heritage of the servants of the LORD, and their righteousness is from Me," says the LORD. (Isaiah 54:17 NKJV)

I used to be prone to having nightmares. I remember one dream in particular; I was in a vehicle with a group of people. There were two men in a car. Both had large guns and were chasing us. We made it to what looked like an old abandoned store and went inside and locked the door. Our hearts were pounding wildly; we all were frightened. Soon the bad guys pulled up and got out of the car, with their guns pointed and ready to shoot us. All of a sudden, the presence of the Lord came over me and reminded me of who I was and that I had power even in my dreams to overcome the enemy. With boldness, I flung open the door, and began shouting to the two men, "Here I am. Now what are you going to do?" As I moved closer and closer to them, I noticed they were backing up away from me with their hands down. Never once did they point their weapons at me. I kept pressing them to answer me, "What do you want?" The two men never said a word. They just turned around, got in their car, and hastily drove off. Before I took action, I had to be reminded that I was a new creature in Christ and that the enemy has no power over me, even when I am sleeping.

> The Israelites ate manna forty years, until they
> came to a land that was settled; they ate manna
> until they reached the border of Canaan. (Exodus
> 16:35 NIV)

As believers, we are still bound to this worldly mentality that everything we need, will cost something monetary. God has demonstrated in his word that he is well able to provide for the needs of his people without using money. As long as the Israelites were in that holding place, called the wilderness, God provided for their every need. God is beyond the word *rich*; he fed two million or more people for forty years without one penny. God the Father, God the Son, and God the Holy Spirit did not need to project how much it would cost to feed millions for five or ten years, not even forty years.

Without anyone's help, God could still be raining down manna from heaven to this day, if he so desired. When God sent Elijah the prophet into hiding (1 Kings 17:2–6), he provided him with water to drink from the brook and food was delivered to Elijah by ravens. These birds delivered to Elijah bread as well as meat, all at no cost to Elijah. Ravens are extremely intelligent and eat an omnivorous (plant and animal) diet. Instead of eating the food for themselves, the ravens obeyed God's command by bringing the food to Elijah. In Genesis 22, God asked Abraham to take his son to the mountain and sacrifice him. Abraham in obedience to God took Isaac to do what God had requested of him. In response to Isaac's question about where the sacrifice was, Abraham said to Isaac that God would provide the lamb for the burnt offering. Seeing Abraham's willingness to obey, God would not allow Abraham to sacrifice his son. Instead, God provided him with a ram to be sacrificed. Because of his obedience, God gave Abraham something that money could not buy—the life of his son Isaac. When we recognize the supremacy of God, that he owns and controls everything in the world, including money, then we are candidates for living the abundant life he has for us. Psalm 24:1 (NIV) says, "The earth is the LORD's, and everything in it, the world, and all who live in it." Whether God chooses to use your wages, bartering, a fish with a coin in its mouth, or even a bird to feed you, you must trust his decision every time.

> The Spirit himself testifies with our spirit that we
> are God's children. (Romans 8:16 NIV)

As children of God, you and I can live here on earth, stress-free, but only if we live as heirs of God. The assurance we have as children of God knows no boundaries, for his assurance goes beyond the things that money can buy. It is as God proclaims—everything belongs to him.

When we settle for living any other way, we forfeit the peace that surpasses all understanding. Perfect peace for the believer in Christ is the peace that spills over into your emotions, causing you to remain at rest when life throws you a curve. Because you have been given an abundance of God's peace, you no longer react to negative situations that have come to bring you down. The peace of God does not have to dissolve when you are facing life-changing events in your life. John 14:27 (NIV) says, "Peace I leave with you; my peace I give you. I do not give to you as the world gives. Do not let your hearts be troubled and do not be afraid." No ordinary human being can receive this peace that comes from the Lord.

We are missing out on God's plan for believers in Christ when we settle for just being an ordinary human being here on earth. For then we are settling for way less than the Lord has paid the price for. Abundant living is receiving from God the things that money cannot buy. Why allow your heart to be troubled and walk in fear, over the things in the earth, that are only temporary in nature? Open your eyes and see, for God has given us something far greater—a forever life.

It has been said that doing the same thing over and over again will always yield the same results. As we discover what abundant living means, we can use this saying to our advantage. We do this by consistently living life from the inside out as God intends for the body of Christ to live here on earth. To live this way on a daily basis (no matter what is going on in the world) ensures we will maintain God's supernatural peace, supernatural provision, and perfect rest. Psalm 91:1 (NIV) says, "Whoever dwells in the shelter of the Most High will rest in the shadow of the Almighty."

Chapter 6

Let This Mind

You will keep him in perfect peace, whose mind
is stayed on you, because he trusts You. (Isaiah
26:3 NKJV)

The prophet Isaiah looked down in the corridor of time and saw
Jesus as our perfect peace. He also saw the stipulation that the
only way we could have this kind of peace was if we keep our
minds fixed on God. We do not like stipulations because they
are usually in the form of some restriction (e.g., "If you rent this
beautiful apartment today, you must lease it for two years, and
you cannot break your lease."). What if you do not like staying
in one place too long? You like the idea of living in this beautiful,
luxurious apartment, but you cannot imagine being tied to it for
two years. After all, you are a wanderer. In the same manner,
Isaiah is saying if you want this peace, then you must trust God
to give it to you as you focus on him.

Yes, you want the perfect peace, but you just cannot seem to
devote that much attention to God, especially in prayer. If your

mind wanders while you are praying, it is a good indication that the flesh has the controlling interest in your mind. The mind thinks nothing of running interference for the flesh when you are communicating with God. The flesh will have your mind thinking on everything from the grocery list to the latest gossip you just heard. Unless something is of an epic nature and it is urgent that you talk to God, your mind will stray away from your current task. It has been linked to the flesh all of its life, including after you got saved. Our spirit alone becomes born again. No other part of us has been renewed. God leaves it up to the individual whether to allow the spirit man to take control of the mind.

> I can do all things through Christ who strengthens me. (Philippians 4:13 NKJV)

It is easier to believe God for this promise when the challenge involves one or more of our five senses. In the physical world, I can do anything I am called to do, because of Christ in me. Since there is no limit in Christ, there is no limit to what we can do. For example, when we have to pass a difficult test to advance in our field of work, we will quote Philippians 4:13. This situation is very easy to believe God for, basically because the knowledge is in me and all I require of the Holy Spirit is to bring it forth from my memory. But what about scriptures that pertain to a complete change in the way we think or the way we process things in our mind? For instance, Philippians 2:5 (NKJV) says: "Let this mind be in you, which was also in Christ Jesus." The word *let* means not to prevent or forbid but allow. The mind of Christ in us can only happen by an act of our will.

When we received Jesus as our Lord and Savior, all of heaven rejoiced. At that moment we received from Jesus everything that belonged to him. Jesus shared with us His Father and His Holy Spirit. He gave us a new nature created in his image, and with it came eternal life. And if that was not enough, he went away to prepare a place for us in heaven to be with him. However, there is one thing that we do not immediately grasp; it is having the mind of Christ. For the most part, our mind is aligned with our flesh. Without it occurring to us that we now have access to Christ's mind, we go right on viewing the word of God as optional. You and I must choose to have his mind and allow the way Christ thinks to become a part of our lives.

The mind is part of the brain that controls our thoughts, emotions, dreams, and also memory. What we think about in every aspect of life is housed right here. Just like your spirit is hidden in your body, God has hidden your mind in your brain. I remember the doctor confirming to me that I was pregnant. At five weeks, I did not look pregnant, but I certainly felt pregnant with morning sickness every day. The only way anyone else knew I was pregnant was by me telling them. As the months went by, it became apparent to all that I was pregnant. Although my baby was growing, he was still hidden from the naked eye. When we become born-again believers in Christ, our spirit man comes alive. However, the mind remains in the same state as before, hidden in our brains, and still subjected to our flesh. In our strength, we cannot command our minds to think as Jesus thinks. Our minds have been conditioned from birth to function in the earth from a human position. But God in his mercy has given us a guaranteed way to let our minds become that of Christ, by giving us His Holy Spirit.

> But very truly I tell you, it is for your good that
> I am going away. Unless I go away, the Advocate
> will not come to you; but if I go, I will send him
> to you. (John 16:7 NIV)

I sometimes wonder what it would look like if, after Jesus was resurrected, he continued living here on earth. Just imagine, two thousand years later, Jesus would still be with us in the flesh. One thing that would be different for believers in Christ is that we would not be filled with the Holy Spirit. We would not have the access we do today to have the mind of Christ. As his disciples, we would be limited in our minds as to what we think and how we think about every detail of life. If Jesus were physically still here, it would be nearly impossible for us to agree on much in the earth. As long as Jesus remained on the earth, we could not share in the way he thinks. In the form of a man, Jesus could only be at one place at a time. As we take a look at the disciples who were with Jesus at the time he walked the earth, we see from the scriptures below that they did not always think like Jesus.

Philip

If you had known Me, you would have known My Father also; from now on you know Him, and have seen Him." Philip said to Him, "Lord, show us the Father, and it is enough for us." Jesus said to him, "Have I been so long with you, and yet you have not come to know Me, Philip? He who has seen Me has seen the Father; how can you say, 'Show us the Father'?" (John 14:7–9 NKJV)

Peter and the other apostles

Peter answered and said to Him, "Even if all are made to stumble because of You, I will never be made to stumble." Jesus said to him, "Assuredly, I say to you that this night, before the rooster crows, you will deny Me three times." Peter said to Him, "Even if I have to die with You, I will not deny You!" And so said all the disciples. (Matthew 26:33–35 NKJV)

The Seventy-Two Disciples

The seventy-two returned with joy and said, "Lord, even the demons submit to us in your name." He replied, "I saw Satan fall like lightning from heaven. I have given you authority to trample on snakes and scorpions and to overcome all the power of the enemy; nothing will harm you. However, do not rejoice that the spirits submit to you, but rejoice that your names are written in heaven." (Luke 10:17–20 NIV)

As we see from the above scriptures, no matter how close Jesus was to his disciples, their thoughts were sometimes far from being heavenly minded. The disciples' thoughts were full of unbelief, pride, and boasting, none of which has ever been found in Jesus. Jesus is the Son of God, who thinks like his Father at all times. Jesus knew what was in man, and he knew how critical it was that man began to think like him. As long as he remained on earth, Jesus knew the man would have an earthly view of spiritual matters. Jesus took the form of a lowly human being so those being saved could become a spiritual being operating in the earth above ordinary human thinking. Jesus never gave in to human reasoning. He remained a spiritual being while here on earth. Jesus knew that humanity was something less than who he was, and he never wavered or forgot his heavenly beginning.

> Take my yoke upon you and learn from me, for I am gentle and humble in heart, and you will find rest for your souls. (Matthew 11:29 NIV)

Upon receiving Jesus as our Savior, we are required to submit ourselves to him and learn of the new nature that has been given unto us. We have to realize that as long as we think more about humanity than our spiritual life, we are functioning at a level below what God intended for us to live. As new creatures in Christ, it is important that we wrap our minds around our new position. People who encountered Jesus recognized that he was one with authority. Jesus's mind was always cohesive with his spirit man. He was more concerned with pleasing the Father than dancing around subjects to avoid offending someone. It was his desire to see everyone come into the truth. Greater works he said we would do. But what exactly are the greater works? How is it possible for believers to perform greater works than Jesus without having a like mind of Christ? The Holy Spirit knows the mind of Christ, and it gives him great pleasure to pass it on to those created in Christ's image. Since we are created in his image, why not think like Jesus? What is stopping you? What is hindering you from having the mind of Christ in your life? Jesus's thoughts were not about bigger, better, and newer things. He tells us in Luke 12:20 about the man who wanted to build bigger barns to store all of his possessions. This man died focusing on things of the earth that were temporary in nature.

> And no one pours new wine into old wineskins. Otherwise, the wine will burst the skins, and both the wine and the wineskins will be ruined. No, they pour new wine into new wineskins. (Mark 2:22 NIV)

An old wineskin cannot be expanded or remolded to accommodate the bubbles and fermentation gasses that are released from the new wine. Therefore, it will burst because the new wine and the old wineskin are not compatible. Our born-again spirit is like the new wine housed in our bodies. When we try to function as new creatures in Christ with our old mind-set (which is conditioned by the world), the results can be just as damaging to the new creature. To continue in our old way of thinking will result in us being at a spiritual standstill, for there is nothing in our old mind-set that wants to obey God. Our old mind-set has been associated with the flesh most of our lives. Some of the results from having an old mind-set are a religious spirit, a critical spirit, a state of confusion, or having a lukewarm nature. The biggest downfall for new creatures in Christ with the same old mind-set is the trivial things in life that we pursue—things such as "my wants, my desires, my dreams, and my goals." To your old mind-set, these things are extremely important to your wellbeing and happiness. All these things are designed to keep us living a self-centered life, which in that state can never bring glory to God.

> Let this mind be in you which was also in Christ
> Jesus. (Philippians 2:5 NKJV)

Our mind should no longer be controlled by our old nature—humanity. As new creatures in Christ, we must understand that God wants us to have a new mind-set. The old mind loves to bring in factors such as reasoning, past experiences, emotions, and feelings. It uses these factors to measure the validity of an idea or concept or whether something is right or wrong. The old mind relies on instincts, hunches, and suspicions instead of the Holy Spirit, who gives us discernment of spirits. The old mind even allows feelings and emotions to determine the effectiveness of a prayer being prayed. That is why some people can go to the altar at church and be prayed for, and at the moment they feel changed. But it is just on the surface where feelings and emotions live. Therefore, it will not last. The mind in its original state can never fully comprehend the depth of the spirit man within. To begin aligning our minds with the mind of Christ, we can start by capturing every thought and making it obey Christ, as we are told to do in 2 Corinthians 10:5.

> When he had received the drink, Jesus said, "It is finished." With that, he bowed his head and gave up his spirit. (John 19:30 NIV)

He traded his life so that many lives could be saved. The prophecies spoken about the plan of God for humanity had come to pass. It is up to each one of us, who has made Jesus Lord of our lives, to live in the manner he prescribes. Jesus has given us permission to let our earthly minds become like his mind. It is finished implies that the door to Jesus's mind is now open, and all who love him are welcome to partake of it. An open invitation has been given to us. Fancy receptions come with a guest list, to which you can only enter if your name appears on the list. The greatest function ever held is the invitation of salvation. Jesus has done away with the exclusive guest list and has invited all to come in and receive him as their Savior. We do not automatically receive the mind of Christ at the moment of salvation. For our thoughts, emotions, dreams, and memories to become like Christ, we must willfully surrender ownership to God. When we allow our minds to be controlled by our spirits, power is then released in the earth; miracles, signs, and wonders are the manifestations. Only when we allow the Holy Spirit to control our spirit by taking hold of our thoughts, emotions, dreams, and even memories; we can then communicate with God the Father, effectively every time.

> And do not be conformed to this world, but be transformed by the renewing of your mind, that you may prove what is that good and acceptable and perfect will of God. (Romans 12:12 NKJV)

Chapter 7

Led by the Spirit

> While they were worshiping the Lord and fasting,
> the Holy Spirit said, "Set apart for me Barnabas
> and Saul for the work to which I have called
> them." (Acts 13:2 NIV)

Extremely remarkable! The Holy Spirit of God talks to us. It is
something that the natural mind cannot process that a person
who is a spirit, whom you cannot see, is living inside of another
person's spirit. But the Holy Spirit has a voice and is very much
alive in all who believe and have accepted Jesus as their Savior.
Since he is the Spirit of the living God, there is much more to
him than just someone who was sent to live in you. Usually, in
elementary school, whenever the teacher leaves the classroom for
more than a few minutes, she or he will select a student to be his
or her eyes and ears while he or she is away. The student's job is
to write down the name of any student who is misbehaving. The
student has no real power or authority to make anyone stop what
they are doing. The only thing this student can do is write the

name of the misbehaving pupil on a piece of paper and give it to the teacher when he or she returns. In the same manner, many believers treat the Holy Spirit as if his only role in their life was to watch over them. But the Holy Spirit is much more than a name taker. Unlike a classmate, the Holy Spirit is not our equal; he is our superior. He is the third member of the Trinity, the Father, the Son, and the Holy Spirit. There is nothing reduced about the Holy Spirit; he is no less than God.

Our ignorance in the reason why he was sent to live in us keeps us from experiencing the full measure of the Holy Spirit's purpose in us. The Holy Spirit has been sent to us with all the authority Jesus possessed when he walked the earth. The Holy Spirit is not in an earthly partnership with us as we know a partnership to be. We know earthly partnerships to be between two or more equals in a business or even a relationship. No, the Holy Spirit lives in us to tell us what to do, when to do it, and how we are to do it. The Holy Spirit's leading is to be in every area of our lives. He never makes suggestions when he speaks; it is always a command. Take a look at the scriptures below, and see a couple of ways the Holy Spirit operates in his position on earth.

> It seemed good to the Holy Spirit and to us not to burden you with anything beyond the following requirements: You are to abstain from food sacrificed to idols, from blood, from the meat of strangled animals and from sexual immorality. You will do well to avoid these things. Farewell. (Acts 15:28–29 NIV)

> Now when they had gone through Phrygia and
> the region of Galatia, they were forbidden by the
> Holy Spirit to preach the word in Asia. After they
> had come to Mysia, they tried to go into Bithynia,
> but the Spirit did not permit them. (Acts 16:6–7
> NKJV)

Notice in Acts 15:28–29 the Holy Spirit has a preference in how believers should govern their lives on earth. With authority in Acts 16:6–7 the Holy Spirit forbade Paul, Silas, and Timothy to preach in Asia, and they were not allowed to go into Bithynia. The Holy Spirit being the Spirit of truth does not speak on his own but speaks what he hears (John 16:13). His function on earth is to be the mouthpiece for God the Father and God the Son. So when the Holy Spirit says in Acts 13:2, "Set apart for me," God is speaking.

Another way the Holy Spirit works is by preparing the body of Christ to walk in holiness and to become flawless before the Lord.

> Husbands, love your wives, just as Christ loved
> the church and gave himself up for her to make
> her holy, cleansing her by the washing with water
> through the word, and to present her to himself as
> a radiant church, without stain or wrinkle or any
> other blemish, but holy and blameless. (Ephesians
> 5:25–27 NIV)

The word *blemish* can be translated as flaws. When we think of flaws, we think of physical flaws, like birth defects, scars from an accident, or genetic flaws. But the type of flaw the scripture above is referring to is the fault or weakness in a person's character. Since we have the Holy Spirit living inside of us, we are without excuse for continuing in character flaws, such as laziness, fits of anger, procrastination, exaggeration, tardiness, and other character traits not listed. The Holy Spirit is perfect, and he brought absolute perfection with him to live inside of us. There is no one more qualified than the Holy Spirit to teach us how to live life in the Spirit.

The Holy Spirit lives in us so that we might adopt his ways and become a person who pleases God. He is the Spirit of perfection, and we are without excuse when we walk in anything that is not like God. We have been endowed by the Holy Spirit, with the ability to walk in the fruit of the Spirit (Galatians 5:22–23) with perfection. We are not being made ready, but we have everything in us to live life right now, with all love, joy, peace, gentleness, goodness, kindness, faithfulness, patience, and self-control. We have been given responsibility to understand that there is nothing missing or broken in the Holy Spirit and with pleasure he shares with us his all. Since we have been given the fruit of Spirit and can no longer plead innocence because of ignorance, according to 2 Corinthians 5:10, we will have to give an account to God for any misuse of it.

> That all of them may be one, Father, just as you
> are in me and I am in you. May they also be in us
> so that the world may believe that you have sent
> me. I have given them the glory that you gave me,

that they may be one as we are one—I in them
and you in me—so that they may be brought to
complete unity. Then the world will know that
you sent me and have loved them even as you have
loved me. (John 17:21–23 NIV)

Here we have the biggest merger ever to take place in history—
not only the largest but also, the most unique merger since time
begin. As each of us received Jesus as our personal Savior, we then
receive the one and only Spirit of God. Because God the Father,
God the Son, and God the Holy Spirit are one, whomever the
Holy Spirit lives in that person becomes one with the Trinity.
Just as Jesus reflected the glory of the Father, when he walked the
earth, we the recipients of the Holy Spirit must also reflect the
glory of the Father. Jesus said in John 17:22 that we have received
the glory to become one with them. Now, because we have already
received the glory, we can become the unified body of Christ as
he intended for us to be.

The Holy Spirit did not come to bring part of God to you
and part to me. The same God now flows in all of us. Ephesians
2:20–22 (NIV) says:

Built on the foundation of the apostles and
prophets, with Christ Jesus himself as the chief
cornerstone. In him the whole building is joined
together and rises to become a holy temple in the
Lord. And in him you too are being built together
to become a dwelling in which God lives by his
Spirit.

Imagine if your home was divided up into several streets in your neighborhood—your bedroom on one street, your kitchen on a different street, your laundry room around the corner from the kitchen, your bathroom two streets over, and your living room down the street from the bathroom. Your everyday life would be laborious, running here and there to take care of your various needs. Thank God our homes are equipped with everything we need under one roof. As it is with our natural house, thank God our spiritual house is connected to God and connected to each other. As one body in Christ, we can stand united in every battle we face on earth and come out victorious. All of us are joined together with one head—Jesus.

Jesus, who is back in heaven, is making arrangements for our permanent move to our heavenly home. In the meantime, he has sent the Holy Spirit as the Spirit of truth to be with us (John 16:12–15). It is imperative that we learn to depend on the leading of the Holy Spirit. Unless we have a paradigm shift in the way we communicate with God, we will miss out on the greatest relationship we could have with him on earth. It is the Holy Spirit's job to make known to the body of Christ that which will bring glory to God. Since the Holy Spirit has a voice, we must not limit ourselves to only receiving from the printed word, the Bible. God has set the precedence on how he wants to communicate with us at any given time. Not only does he talk to us through the Bible, but he also speaks to us by his Spirit. Most of us have been guilty from time to time of giving credit to something other than the Holy Spirit. For instance, "Something told me to go here," or "I should have followed my first mind." Some have even given credit to feelings: "I had a feeling I should have gone the other way." But what about given credit to where credit is due—the Holy Spirit?

I remember the first time I was introduced to the voice of the Holy Spirit. My husband and I were not born-again Christians when we were married. Not only that, but we knew that I was unable to have children. A couple of years later, I became a believer and fell in love with Jesus. I told God, shortly after my conversion, that if I never had children, I was glad that I got to know him. That was all God wanted from me, to love him with all my heart. And so, word came from heaven, and the Holy Spirit relayed the message to me. One night while sleeping I had a vision. I saw a giant hand coming down toward me, touching my abdomen area. Then I heard a voice, the Holy Spirit, saying to me, "Now, your womb is open." Remember, the Holy Spirit will tell you of things to come (John 16:13). At that moment, without any doubt, I knew the necessary surgery had been performed on me, and I would become pregnant one day.

Before that night, I had read about the women in the Bible like Isaac's mother Sarah, Samson's mother, Samuel's mother and Elizabeth, John the Baptist's mother. These women had one thing in common; they were all barren and then God healed them. Though I was encouraged to read their stories, still they all were just stories in the Bible to me. My situation did not change, until that night when I received a personal word from God. Month after month, for over a year, I clung to faith in the word I received from God. True to his word, without any assistance from medical science, I became pregnant with our firstborn.

We are blessed in America to have an unlimited number of Bibles, be it hard copies, the Internet, or Bible apps on your phone. But what if access to Bibles was suddenly taken away from you? What would you do then? Hopefully that will never happen. But God gave you and me someone that no one can ever take from us—the Holy Spirit. We have living in us God the Spirit, who is in constant communication with God in heaven. Therefore, we have access to God twenty-four hours a day, through the Holy Spirit. There are some religions that have altered the Bible to satisfy their needs. Even well-meaning believers can take a scripture out of context to suit their lifestyle. However, there is no way anyone can alter the Holy Spirit in the believer's life. The Holy Spirit only speaks the truth, and be assured, he wants us to understand him fully. As Jesus is the same, yesterday, today, and forever, so is the Holy Spirit. I thank God for the Bible, for it is his love letter written to us. The Bible is a necessary part of our relationship with God, as the scriptures below point out to us.

> For everything that was written in the past was written to teach us, so that through the endurance taught in the Scriptures and the encouragement they provide we might have hope. (Romans 15:4 NIV)

> All Scripture is God-breathed and is useful for teaching, rebuking, correcting and training in righteousness, so that the servant of God may be thoroughly equipped for every good work. (2 Timothy 3:16–17 (NIV)

As much as we need the written word of God in our lives, intimacy with the Holy Spirit is much more needed. It is the Holy Spirit who leads and guides into all truth, for his name's sake. The Holy Spirit lives in us to keep you and me from having a defeated life by living on our five senses, and from always looking for reason to make sense out of something unexplainable. When Jesus was on the earth, he was the light of the world. Now, the light of the world lives in every believer who is born again. It is the Holy Spirit's turn to shine through us as that bright light from heaven.

> Those who live according to the flesh have their minds set on what the flesh desires; but those who live in accordance with the Spirit have their minds set on what the Spirit desires. The mind governed by the flesh is death, but the mind governed by the Spirit is life and peace. (Romans 8:5–6 NIV)

Chapter 8

Set Apart

And do this, understanding the present time: The hour has already come for you to wake up from your slumber, because our salvation is nearer now than when we first believed. The night is nearly over; the day is almost here. So let us put aside the deeds of darkness and put on the armor of light. (Romans 13:11–12 NIV)

As my retirement date from my job drew near, I was anticipating getting started on my short to-do list. The first thing on the to-do list was to give my alarm clock a break; after thirty-plus years, it too deserved to be retired. Sometimes I would slap the snooze button, at least, five times before I would drag myself out of the bed. But like all things in life, eventually, the thing we are waiting for will come to pass. Paul is saying in Romans 13 to all believers that it is time for us to wake up and understand that the day of Lord's appearing is near and in fact, is almost here. It is time for all who are born-again Christians to put away the things that make them look and act just like the world. Just as I would sometimes repeatedly hit the snooze button before finally getting out of bed, we sometimes hang on to the things in this world too long after we get saved. Sooner or later, if I wanted to keep my job, I had to get up, get ready, and go to work. As believers in Christ, we too are only delaying the inevitable by continuing in darkness. We must retire any deed that does not fit into the plans God have for our lives. The time has come for all believers to live life as full-blooded new creatures in Christ, rather than living like an ordinary human being, for we have been set apart to do the things God has prepared for us to do.

There are no gray areas in God. Therefore, we must put aside every area in our life that we consider to be a gray area. God is either for something or against it; there is never an in between for him. For instance, in Romans 13:13, it says, "Let us behave decently." This implies to God's standard of decency rather than the world's standard of decency. Decency means polite, acceptable, moral, honest, or good behavior and attitudes that show respect for others. As we know, the world's standard of decency has been on a downward spiral for years. What is being shown on television today is a good indication of how far society has gotten away from wholesome moral values. Also, people are driven by their own opinions; they have little to no respect for authority, or the lives of others.

Since God's word never changes, we can no longer afford to let anything or anyone ransack the life we now live, for it can never bring glory to God. Living for Jesus must dominate every aspect of your life, your mind, your will, your emotions, and your thought life, including your secret desires. How to serve God with your whole heart and mind should trump everything else in your life. This way of thinking is the most important aspect of your life because it is what sets you apart as a child of God. Psalm 4:3 (NKJV) says, "But know that the LORD has set apart for Himself him who is godly; the LORD will hear when I call to Him." You must guard this way of thinking and not allow darkness to set in and try to extinguish the light in you. As we focus our attention on being set apart for God, we have to allow him to expose every habit in our lives that does not bring glory to him.

I used to smoke a pack of cigarettes a day, and it was by far the strongest addiction in my life. I tried many times to quit on my own, only to go right back to smoking. The least little thing that aggravated me would set me off running back to the cigarettes. Even after I came to know Jesus as my Savior, I still smoked. It was not till I was pregnant with my firstborn that I was able to wean myself off of cigarettes and quit early on in my pregnancy. After the birth of my son, I went back to smoking a few cigarettes per day. Eventually I quit smoking again.

My husband was fired from his job the day before I was scheduled for a C-section with our second child. As you can imagine, it was a terrible blow to the both of us. A few weeks later, my friend who was strong in her faith was diagnosed with a terrible disease. My husband was still without a job, and I was at this point without hope, so I picked up a cigarette and started back smoking. This time, it was very short lived. A couple of days later, while I was smoking a cigarette, all of a sudden, the inside of my body was on fire; I was in terrible pain. My three-year-old helped me from the dining room to the sofa in the living room. The burning in me lasted a few minutes, and all I could do was cry, repent, and ask God to forgive me. The fire stopped as suddenly as it had started. From that day forward, I have been set free from cigarettes, and I have never experienced that burning again. No more smoking for me in the time of trouble. There have been plenty of occasions to light up, but the desire has never come back.

As the word of God says, "He who the Son sets free, is free indeed." In other words, no one who has been called out of darkness by Jesus need ever be in bondage to anything here on earth. Having Christ as the master of your life means freedom. No longer are we to struggle in any area that he has paid the price so we can become as he was here on earth. If we are to be as he was, then, it is critical for all believers to follow his example by giving up all rights to our habits and addictions that do not bring God glory. John 8:12 (NIV) says, "When Jesus spoke again to the people, he said, 'I am the light of the world. Whoever follows me will never walk in darkness, but will have the light of life.'" If we fail in any area of our life as new creatures in Christ, then it is to our shame that we have allowed something to take place in our heart that should not be there. What is it that keeps you from displaying Jesus who is the light of life in you? Why do we hold on to harmful things in our lives just because, somewhere in our flesh we like it? We can be guilty of putting too much importance in identifying with others as well, especially our relatives and friends.

> While Jesus was still talking to the crowd, his
> mother and brothers stood outside, wanting to
> speak to him. Someone told him, "Your mother
> and brothers are standing outside, wanting to
> speak to you." He replied to him, "Who is my
> mother, and who are my brothers?" Pointing to
> his disciples, he said, "Here are my mother and
> my brothers. For whoever does the will of my
> Father in heaven is my brother and sister and
> mother." (Matthew 12:46–50 NIV)

How would you have reacted if you were Jesus's mother,
brother, or sister and heard him saying his disciples were his
family? To most of us, there are no relationships more important
in our lives than that of our immediate family. However, Jesus
came to set a new precedence, something that had never been
done on earth before. Jesus knew he was not here on earth to hold
on to his earthly relationships. Jesus was saying, "I know why I
am here, and I know who sent me here. I can only do the will of
my Father and include everyone who catches the Father's vision so
that they can become part of our family." Everyone is invited, no
matter their race, creed, color, or background. Nothing mattered
more to Jesus than fulfilling the will of his Father.

Not following the example that Christ has set before us means
we are putting our relationship with our earthly family members
before the responsibility we have to follow Jesus. It also says we
have not fully grasped the meaning of what it means to be adopted
into the family of God. In John 13:14 NIV, Jesus tells his disciples,

"Now that I, your Lord and Teacher, have washed your feet, you also should wash one another's feet." In other words, what you see Jesus doing, you must also do. What you hear him saying, you must say. If your love one is not saved, you should not follow them into anything that leads you into sin. You must be willing to separate yourself from them to be like Jesus. Jesus said, "Whoever does the will of my Father in heaven is my family member." The goal in life for all of Jesus's family members must be the same: to do the will of our mutual Father.

In John 11, Jesus received a message that his friend Lazarus was sick unto death, yet he lingered and allowed him to die. From a human perspective, he was not a good friend of Lazarus. If he were, he would have rushed to his side and saved him from death. Or he could have just sent the word as in Matthew 8:8 and healed him as he had done for the centurion's servant. Jesus, the Son of God, did nothing to prevent his friend from dying. Jesus allowed Lazarus to die because nothing was more important to him than bringing glory to God. Jesus used every opportunity to glorify His Father in heaven. He used the moment with Lazarus to showcase the power His Father had given him. This demonstration brought great glory to God.

We must use every opportunity to bring glory to God our Father. Are there any relationships in your life that do not bring God glory? Then, this relationship is displeasing to God and can never bring him glory in its current state. Here is where loving God more than others comes into play in your life. You have to terminate the relationship. Second Corinthians 6:17–18 (NKJV) says:

> Therefore "Come out from among them and be
> separate, says the Lord. Do not touch what is
> unclean, and I will receive you. I will be a Father
> to you, and you shall be My sons and daughters,
> says the LORD Almighty."

God has raised the bar for all those who have been set apart to live life on earth as his sons and daughters. He is very conditional about who we can and cannot be in a relationship with. If we choose to ignore his command to separate ourselves from all unclean relationships, then this shows that our loyalties are misplaced.

> You are of *your* father the devil, and the desires of
> your father you want to do. He was a murderer
> from the beginning, and does not stand in the
> truth, because there is no truth in him. When he
> speaks a lie, he speaks from his own *resources,* for
> he is a liar and the father of it. (John 8:44 NKJV)

Perhaps the biggest change that you and I will have to make if we are to be truly set apart and fit for the Master's use is to break all connections with the devil. As long as we operate from our flesh, we are connected with the devil. Galatians 5:17 (NIV) says, "For the flesh desires what is contrary to the Spirit, and the Spirit what is contrary to the flesh. They are in conflict with each other so that you are not to do whatever you want." Satan is the father of lies. Just as the serpent talked Eve into partaking of the forbidden fruit, he charms our flesh into things that are contrary to the Spirit. Satan is the owner of a vast arsenal of junk. Everything bad and evil belongs to him.

Satan is the master deceiver, and our flesh being weak buys into his deception again and again. Why would anyone who is a born-again believer in Christ want anything from Satan? First Corinthians 6:9–10 (NIV) says, "Or do you not know that wrongdoers will not inherit the kingdom of God? Do not be deceived: Neither the sexually immoral nor idolaters nor adulterers nor men who have sex with men nor thieves nor the greedy nor drunkards nor slanderers nor swindlers will inherit the kingdom of God." This scripture is one of the many that shows some of the junk Satan entices our flesh with and the consequences we face when we give in to it. For further reading see Galatians 5:19–21, 1 Corinthians 10:6, Ephesians 4:30–32, and 1 Peter 4:15.

Our only recourse is to come clean with God. We must stop living in denial. If you and I know that there is something or some things in our lives that hinder us from being truly set apart, from looking like Jesus in all that we do, now is the time to confess it. I have been guilty of more than one of the ungodly characteristics listed in the referenced scriptures above. Thank God, you and I have an Advocate who is interceding for us, even now. And thank God, we can repent, confess our sins, and know that God has cleansed us from all unrighteousness.

> If we say that we have no sin, we are deceiving
> ourselves and the truth is not in us. If we confess
> our sins, He is faithful and righteous to forgive us

our sins and to cleanse us from all unrighteousness. If we say that we have not sinned, we make Him a liar and His word is not in us. (1 John 1:8–10 NKJV)

Chapter 9

Standing Firm

> Therefore, my dear brothers and sisters, stand firm. Let nothing move you. Always give yourselves fully to the work of the Lord, because you know that your labor in the Lord is not in vain. (1 Corinthians 15:58 NIV)

Standing firm in the Lord in the midst of a trial can be difficult. Sometimes it is very hard to see your way to the other side of the situation. There was a period when my husband and I were struggling financially. It seemed the only thing that was going right in our finances was that we were united in tithing. We have never wavered as to who the 10 percent of the income belonged to—God. One stressful time in particular after we had given our tithe and we paid the urgent bills that were due, we had about thirty dollars left for the week. With our two kids in private school and four mouths to feed, plus gas to put in the vehicle, we were in a crunch. How were thirty dollars going to last us until the next pay day? During that time, I walked the floors and prayed a lot.

One day while I was walking and praying, I became tired of standing, so I stopped. I began to laugh uncontrollably and said, "Lord, how exactly do you want me to stand (physically I meant)?" The harder I laughed, the stronger I began to feel not only spiritually, but emotionally and physically as well. My legs found strength, as if a huge weight was lifted off of me. I was reminded of Nehemiah 8:10 (NIV) where it says, "For the joy of the Lord is your strength." That day was a breaking point for me as I began to understand that you must stand firm in your heart and not lose your joy, regardless of your circumstances. The enemy loves nothing better than to see us struggle and get weighed down with our problems. God got us through that week, and I learned to stand a little stronger in my faith as a result of having been tested. Many more tests have come since then, financial, relational, even sickness, but after each test I have learned to stand firmer in my faith.

> For in the gospel the righteousness of God is revealed—a righteousness that is by faith from first to last, just as it is written: "The righteous will live by faith." (Romans 1:17 NIV)

We do not know the strength that God has provided for us until we have walked through the difficulty. No, we do not know when or where trouble will arise, but we do know that everything we need to endure has been provided for us by the Lord. When a tropical storm's wind speed reaches seventy-five miles per hour, it is known as a hurricane it this part of the world. Being from south Louisiana, I have experienced quite a few hurricanes, Andrew, Rita, Gustav, and the infamous Katrina, among others. Thank God we are given enough time to prepare ourselves for the impending hurricane. Most of us do just that: go to the store and purchase the necessary items needed, like batteries, flashlights, canned foods, water, etc. We board up windows and remove items in the yard that can be easily carried away by the storm. After all is done, we settle down and wait and pray for God's mercy. Having done all that we can do, we can be at peace, because it is all left in God's hand. That is exactly how God would have us to respond to the trials that come our way. His words say, "Let nothing move you." Yes, the storm is coming, but you have taken the necessary steps needed to weather the storm. By putting on the whole armor of God, you will be able to overcome every trick of the enemy. Ephesians 6:10–11 (NIV) says, "Finally, be strong in the Lord and his mighty power. Put on the full armor of God, so that you can take your stand against the devil's schemes."

Without proper understanding, you and I will continue to allow life's circumstances to move us out of the standing firm position God has set in place for us. When you trust God with all your heart, it becomes a protective barrier around your entire being—your mind, body, and spirit. This barrier enables you to stand firm and allows you to overcome all the fiery darts of the enemy. When Daniel was accused by his enemies of dishonoring the king, he was put inside of a lion's den to be eaten by the lions. Daniel's only recourse was to stand firm and trust God with his life. The next morning, the king frantically ran to see if Daniel survived the lion's den. Daniel replied, in Daniel 6:21–22 (NIV), "May the king live forever! My God sent his angel, and he shut the mouths of the lions. They have not hurt me, because I was found innocent in his sight. Nor have I ever done any wrong before you, Your Majesty." When trouble comes to you by way of sickness, financial upheaval, or confusion brought on by the enemy, you must learn to rest and trust God completely. Nothing the enemy sends our way can ever move us from our heavily guarded position.

> Trust in the Lord with all your heart and lean not on your own understanding; in all your ways submit to him, and he will make your paths straight. (Proverbs 3:5–6 NIV)

In the world of the firefighters, each alarm is preceded by a number, (i.e., one alarm, two alarm, up to five alarm). The number measures the severity of the fire. The higher the number of the alarm, the more fire trucks, fire equipment, firefighters, etc., are needed to extinguish the fire. The fire stations have to be prepared to fight any level of fire. If the alarm is high enough, it includes calling in off-duty firefighters. Regardless of how the fire was started, the battle is waged against the fire, and the goal is to defeat it by putting it out. When we give ourselves fully to the work of the Lord, it means we must stay ready to work as if it was a five-alarm fire. Every time firefighters prepare for a fire, the must put on their firefighter gear, which weighs about forty-five pounds. If the gear gets wet, it adds more weight to it. Plus, if the firefighter carries equipment, such as radios, flashlights, or heavy duty tools, the extra weight becomes seventy pounds or more. Thank God there are dedicated men and women who serve us in this capacity, for that is a lot of extra weight to carry. The good news for us as believers in Christ is that God has simplified our gear by putting everything we need inside of us. There is no additional gear needed in the event of a fire. All we have to do is stand firm and use our equipment found within us.

> Stand firm then, with the belt of truth buckled around your waist, with the breastplate of righteousness in place, and with your feet fitted with the readiness that comes from the gospel of peace. In addition to all this, take up the shield of faith, with which you can extinguish all the flaming arrows of the evil one. Take the helmet of salvation and the sword of the Spirit, which is the word of God. (Ephesians 6:14–17 NIV)

Our life assignment from the Lord is not the same as the vocation we have selected to do in this world. The work we have selected to do as our vocation has a retirement date, where we stop working on the job and move into the retirement phase of our lives. But when it comes to our life assignment, there is no retirement date. John 9:4 (NIV) says, "As long as it is day, we must do the works of him who sent me. Night is coming, when no one can work." The ultimate mission is to win souls and make disciples, but God has given to each of us a unique assignment to complete the mission. Therefore, we are to seek the Lord and discover what he would have us to do specifically.

> Now the word of the LORD came to me saying, *"Before I formed you in the womb I knew you, And before you were born I consecrated you; I have appointed you a prophet to the nations."* Then I said, "Alas, Lord GOD! Behold, I do not know how to speak, Because I am a youth." (Jeremiah 1:4–6 NIV)

As a child, I always thought I would grow up to become a teacher. When I took a different educational path, I just assumed it was not meant to be. Little did I know years later that God would confirm me by saying, "You are a teacher." He did not mean in the education system but as a teacher in the body of Christ. Eventually, I began to lead small group meetings, weekly Bible studies, and teaching on retreats. A few years later, God got even more specific with me one day, and he said, "I want you to write books." He began to tell me what genre of books I would be writing as well as the targeted audience. Now, I must admit, I had a Jeremiah moment, where I did not think I was qualified to write a book, let alone multiple books. Like Jeremiah, God knew us before we were in our mother's womb. God does not qualify us according to our background, age, education, or any of the things that would disqualify us by the world's standard. When God speaks into our lives, he has already looked at our hearts and knows our willingness to obey him. The assignment that God has given us to do is the primary reason we exist here on earth. When we understand our purpose for being here and begin to work on our assignment, we know that as long as we stand firm in Christ, we will not fail.

> For we are God's handiwork, created in Christ
> Jesus to do good works, which God prepared in
> advance for us to do. (Ephesians 2:10 NIV)

Chapter 10

The Living Way

There is a way that seems right to a man, but its
end is the way of death. (Proverbs 14:12 NKJV)

Have you ever found yourself doing something when in your
heart you knew that God did not approve of your actions? What
can you possibly gain in this world by doing what you believe is
right even though it goes against the will of God? As believers in
Christ, the only thing we will find at the end of our self-made
journey is destruction and death. God is counting on us to see
the big picture, which is living life on earth according to the
leading of the Holy Spirit. It should not look like the road the lost
is traveling. We must understand and accept the absolute truth,
which is all roads (no exceptions) traveled by unbelievers lead to
death, followed by hell. It is the Holy Spirit alone who knows the
ins and outs of the road we are to travel.

We know that anyone born of God does not
continue to sin; the One who was born of God

keeps them safe, and the evil one cannot harm them. (1 John 5:18 NIV)

One thing we can be sure of is the enemy is always laying traps for us, hoping we will take the bait by falling into sin. It is the sin that lurks in our minds that keep us at risk of falling prey to the enemy's plan. But when you take on the mind of Christ, you are saying, "No matter how tempting it is, I will not give in." It is having the mind of Christ that will keep you strong and rooted in the word of God. This way God's word becomes supreme in your life and is all you need to defeat the devil and the world in which you live. As you crucify your flesh by having a mind makeover, your feelings have less of a chance to dominate your emotions. Other people's opinion will no longer have the same effect on you as it did before. You will become dead to those words that are meant to hurt you or cause you to doubt God. Your desire now is to please God above all else, even if it means losing friendships, family, status, or popularity among your peers.

> And I, brethren, could not speak to you as to spiritual people but as to carnal, as to babes in Christ. I fed you with milk and not with solid food; for until now you were not able to receive it, and even now you are still not able; for you are still carnal. For where there are envy, strife, and divisions among you, are you not carnal and behaving like mere men? (1 Corinthians 3:1–3 NKJV)

The most dangerous relationships for the believer can be other believers who are not walking in the Spirit, but in the flesh, the ones the Bible calls carnal believers. A carnal believer is someone whose acts, and his or her deeds are outside of the spiritual realm and are mainly seen as fleshy. They will only accept you as long as you are catering more to your flesh by loving this world and all the pleasures it provides for people. The moment you begin to show signs of having the mind of Christ and begin forsaking the pleasures of this world, you begin to disturb the carnal believer. They will see something different about you that shows up their carnality. As a result, they are unable to relate to you now because they are still living in the flesh. However, God has put inside of you the ability always to do what is right, even if everyone around you is pressuring you to do what is wrong. Jude 24 (NKJV) says, "Now to Him who is able to keep you from stumbling, And to present you faultless." Jude is not saying that you will not stumble ever again, but that God is well able to keep you walking upright forever. It is, however, up to us to grasp the meaning that God has given us a new way of living. And by following the lead of the Holy Spirit, our lives can be filled with all righteousness all the time.

> Therefore, there is now no condemnation for those who are in Christ Jesus, because through Christ Jesus the law of the Spirit who gives life has set you free from the law of sin and death. (Romans 8:1–2 NIV)

Yes, the struggle is real, but it becomes a victory for the believer when we discover that we now have the backing of all of heaven behind us. God has given us the upper hand in combating the flesh that fights against the spirit. It becomes clear to us that the price Jesus paid on Calvary was for our total healing and that it also includes the renewal of our minds. It is from this new mind-set that we allow our spirit within to control our minds. When we take into account, it is our God-given right to have the mind of Christ; we can no longer afford to have our flesh dictate to our mind how life will be for us. If we renounce the flesh and say yes to the spirit, the freedom that God has proclaimed as ours will become evident in our lives.

> Jesus said to him, "I am the way, the truth, and the life. No one comes to the Father except through Me." (John 14:7 NKJV)

Jesus makes the bold claim that states there is no other way. He is the absolute truth and the only one who can give life to you. This statement made by Jesus is as clear as it gets in saying that there can never be a substitute for coming to the Father. Jesus did not mix words, and if we fail to recognize any part of his confession, then we are living a lie and will be subject to God's wrath. Let us take a look at the way, the truth, and the life in John 14:7 and see how it applies to our way of thinking.

The Way

> That if you confess with your mouth the Lord Jesus and believe in your heart that God has

raised Him from the dead, you will be saved. (Romans 10:9 NKJV)

My daughter Kristen has a great sense of direction. We first discovered how skilled she was when we were on vacation in Tennessee; she was about eight years old at the time. My husband, James, was driving back to the hotel we were staying at, and neither he nor I could remember how to get back. It was then we discovered Kristen's keen sense of direction as she guided us back to the hotel by remembering scenery and buildings. Once upon a time, wise men followed a star to locate baby Jesus. When my children were younger, James and I relied on maps and highway signs for directions when we traveled. Today, most of us mainly rely on the GPS to get us to our destination. Travel guidance may come and go, but the word of the Lord is here to stay.

There are a few things in life that will remain a constant in the earth, the way humans are born; all humans will die, and there is only one way to be saved from our sins. Jesus is the gateway we must travel to arrive at the desired final destination we all long to see—heaven. It does not matter what belief a person of celebrity status proclaims as the way to everlasting bliss; the result will be the same every time: disappointment and eternal damnation for those who follow them. We must settle in our hearts and minds that any religion that does not confess that Jesus is Lord is false. Allow yourself to take this word from Jesus *(I am the way)* and meditate on it day and night until it becomes an absolute truth to you. Once this word becomes real to you, you will never buy into the lie of the world that there are many ways to God. When Jesus says, "I am the way," that means no one can truthfully proclaim that God has given them permission to expand the door that leads to him.

The Truth

> The entirety of Your word is truth, and every one of Your righteous judgments endures forever. (Psalm 119:160 NKJV)

Based on the truth that Jesus Christ is the Son of God, every promise he has made will come to pass. Jesus says in John 17:17 (NKJV), "Sanctify them by Your truth, Your word is truth." Because we have accepted that he is the only way, we can know that God has made us holy and pure in his sight. As we allow our minds to focus on Jesus being the truth, we can overcome every false way that leads away from God's word. There are sayings that we use today that have no biblical basis, yet they are often quoted as if it was taken from the Bible. For instance, "Cleanliness is next to godliness." The truth according to the word of God is not found in this saying. A person can be squeaky clean on the outside and have a very ungodly character in the inside. Cleanliness applies to your outward being while godliness means to have a great reverence for God or to be a godly person. Without knowing the truth as the Lord would have us to know, we will go on thinking that somewhere in the Bible this statement lies.

The Life

> Furthermore, tell the people, "This is what the
> Lord says: See, I am setting before you the way of
> life and the way of death." (Jeremiah 21:8 NIV)

Always gracious, God refuses to dictate to us which way to choose. If we are to follow God and choose life, then our minds must follow suit. To have this life of God alive inside of us and to pass over his viewpoint of living is foolishness on the believer's part, for no man can say that he belongs to God and still hold on to his old way of living. The new life we now live must look like the life Jesus lived while he was on earth. As we give up our old way of living, we become embedded with the mind of Christ and solely controlled by his way of thinking. Our perspective about living life gradually changes as we embrace God's viewpoint. With great determination to be like Jesus, we will begin to say this life is not my own. Having crucified your flesh and renewed your mind, you are well on your way to a life that is well pleasing to God and with the assurance that you are now in his perfect will.

> As obedient children, not conforming yourselves
> to the former lusts, as in your ignorance; but as
> He who called you is holy, you also be holy in all
> your conduct, 16 because it is written, "Be holy,
> for I am holy." (1 Peter 1:14–16 NKJV)

Chapter 11

Fear God Only

> So do not fear, for I am with you; do not be dismayed, for I am your God. I will strengthen you and help you; I will uphold you with my righteous right hand. (Isaiah 41:10 NIV)

What is the first thing that comes to your mind when you hear the word *dictator*? A mean, ill-tempered, cruel, brutal, and nasty person, right? Or perhaps someone who rules a country with an iron fist. Count your blessings if you were born in a country where democracy is the rule. However, you may have physically been born in a country under democracy, but spiritually we all have been birthed into a dictatorship kingdom—the kingdom of God. The Lord says in Isaiah 45:5 (NIV), "I am the LORD, and there is no other; apart from me there is no God." While our heavenly Father is a dictator, none of the above adjectives used to describe earthly dictators applies to him. God is not a dictator over one country. No, he rules as Lord over the world and beyond with absolute authority. Matthew 28:18 (NIV) says, "Then Jesus came to them and said, 'All authority in heaven and on earth has been given to me.'" Knowing this, we still choose to walk in fear about everything except God.

What makes fear so powerful that we tend to forget in times of trouble the promises of God? All of heaven is on your side because God is for you. No matter what negative force tries to come your way, God is right there. God is not moved, nor is he ever taken by surprise. If we were to walk in the darkest night of our life, God would still be there to guide us safely through to the other side. Fear is a distressing emotion aroused by impending danger, evil, pain, etc. It is a taxation on your emotions that grips the heart and holds the mind hostage to the thought that something bad is going to happen. Whether the threat is real or imagined, it has the same effect on us every time.

Most of my fears followed me over into my new life in Christ. I feared speaking before an audience, snakes, and anything that crawled on its belly like a snake, especially a stinging caterpillar. However, nothing frightened me more than having to drive while it is raining, thundering, and lightning. Years ago, I was at work, sitting at my desk, looking out the window, and a thunderstorm appeared seemingly out of nowhere. It was filled with dark clouds, rain, thunder, and lightning. Of course, I was frightened, but worse than that, it was almost time for me to get off from work and pick my children up from school. I had never been late picking my kids up from school. Did I panic? Yes! But I began talking to the Lord, as I usually do, telling him (as if he didn't already know) all my fears and troubles. Then, something amazing happened that changed my life and how I viewed thunderstorms. God said to me and demonstrated at the same time, "I will stop the rain for you." While he was talking, the rain stopped, the dark clouds left, and the sun came back out. When I realized that God loved me so much and cared about the things that concerned me, it made thunderstorms small in my eyes, and the fear was gone. Praise God!

> And he said to Him, "All these things I will give You, if You fall down and worship me." Then Jesus said to him, "Go, Satan! For it is written, 'YOU SHALL WORSHIP THE LORD YOUR GOD, AND SERVE HIM ONLY.'" Then the devil left Him; and behold, angels came and began to minister to Him. (Matthew 4:9–11 NKJV)

When the humanity in you recognizes that you are also a spiritual being, it changes the whole game. For now, you know beyond a shadow of a doubt that nothing is more powerful than God. And if God is for you (and he is), nothing by any means shall harm you in this life. Instead of being the fearful person who is moved by what he or she sees and hears, you become a powerful force that the enemy sees as someone he cannot bully. You begin living your life like you know the word of God is true. Psalm 91:5–7 (NIV) says: You will not fear the terror of night, nor the arrow that flies by day, nor the pestilence that stalks in the darkness, nor the plague that destroys at midday. A thousand may fall at your side, ten thousand at your right hand, but it will not come near you. Though the enemy can no longer bully you, he will attempt to keep you bound in your mind to the memory of things that caused fear in you.

One year my family and I were vacationing in San Antonio and decided to attend a local church that Sunday. The pastor issued a challenge to the congregation, which was to do something that you would not ordinarily do. Little did I know that I would have an opportunity to meet that challenge that day. My husband and children love theme park rides, so we went to Sea World after church. As for me, I am always the one sitting down holding everyone else's belongings. Any ride that dropped, jerked, twisted, turned your body upside down, or moved at a very high rate of speed scared me.

After my family had ridden a particular one that they all said was "not so scary," my husband encouraged me to get on the ride with him. I remembered the words of the pastor, and I said, "Why not? I will do it." My family was pretty excited. I, on the other hand, was still a little apprehensive. I still had the memory of the last ride I got on years ago that scared me so that it turned me against all rides. But from the moment I got on the ride, my husband gently coached me through it. He told me what was about to happen before it would happen, right to the end of the ride. If it were not for my husband being by my side, I probably would have panicked, even though this particular ride was pretty harmless. Just like my husband was with me that day, God is with us every step of the way, even when we want to give in to fear. He is right there encouraging us to be not afraid and to be not dismayed, for he is our God.

> Then the church throughout Judea, Galilee
> and Samaria enjoyed a time of peace and was
> strengthened. Living in the fear of the Lord and
> encouraged by the Holy Spirit, it increased in
> numbers. (Acts 9:31 NIV)

The secret to a successful life as a believer in Christ is to live with the fear of the Lord as your compass. As Acts 9:31 says, we will experience joy, peace, strength, growth, and absolute encouragement from the Holy Spirit. The fear of the Lord is you understanding that he is with you, and where he is, his presence will always be magnified, bigger than your life and everything around you. With God with you, it is pointless for you to be afraid. When we fear others, it equates to doubting God is right there with you.

> I tell you, my friends, do not be afraid of those
> who kill the body and after that can do no more.
> But I will show you whom you should fear: Fear
> him who, after the killing of the body, has power
> to throw you into hell. Yes, I tell you, fear him.
> (Luke 12:4–5 NIV)

The fear of the Lord for us must go deeper than the surface of our minds. It must become a knowing in our spirit, just like you know in your spirit that you are saved and on your way to heaven. As believers in Christ, we must hold fast to the truth that something good has already happened to us the moment we gave our hearts to the Lord. Because of this truth, we can now say as Paul says in Romans 8:31, "If God is for us, who can be against us." It is because of this knowledge that God is for us, that we can give him the reverence he so richly deserves.

As new creatures in Christ, it is not in our spirit to fear anything or anyone else but to fear God only. It is our carnal way of thinking that keeps us from reverencing God in the manner he deserves. Second Samuel 6:6 (NIV) says: When they came to the threshing floor of Nakon, Uzzah reached out and took hold of the ark of God, because the oxen stumbled. The Lord's anger burned against Uzzah because of his irreverent act; therefore, God struck him down, and he died there beside the ark of God.

A seeming innocence act by Uzzah brought instant judgment against him by God that cost him his life. To carelessly assume that you are doing something out of reverence for God can prove to be quite costly. In all we do or say, we must find out what the Lord requires in the matter.

> "No weapon formed against you shall prosper, and every tongue which rises against you in judgment You shall condemn. This is the heritage of the servants of the Lord, and their righteousness is from Me," says the Lord. (Isaiah 54:17 NKJV)

As a servant of the Lord, every weapon that is formed against you begins in the spirit realm. By the time it reaches you, it looks natural—for instance, someone starting a rumor about you, and it does not have an ounce of truth in it. Where did that come from? Or someone coming up to you and insulting you, in hopes of picking a fight with you. Who instigated that? The things we go through in the natural have greater meaning in the spiritual realm. The devil recognizes more than we do how protected we are on the earth. He knows that we generally try to make things fit into the natural realm. Now to keep us grounded, there will always be some religious person to aid our thinking of natural thoughts and inform us that we are just human beings. Let's do a two for one here and give back to the devil and the religious crowd. John 4:24 (NKJV) says, "God is Spirit, and those who worship Him must worship in spirit and truth." If God is a Spirit, then how can I truly worship him if I am merely a human being?

Just like marriage is between a man and woman, our relationship with God is between God the Spirit and our inner being, which is a spirit. We must choose to walk in the Spirit. When we spiritualize the life we live, it keeps us one step ahead of the enemy. Ephesians 6:12 (NKJV) says, "For we do not wrestle against flesh and blood, but against principalities, against powers, against the rulers of the darkness of this age, against spiritual hosts of wickedness in the heavenly places." As human beings, we are unable to fight against the forces in high places, for we cannot fight something we cannot see. The enemy brings it to us in the natural realm, in hopes that we fight in the natural and lose sight of who we really are, therefore losing the battle. When we walk in the Spirit, we do not panic because we recognize the enemy, and we use the weapons that have been provided for us.

> For the weapons of our warfare are not carnal
> but mighty in God for pulling down strongholds,
> casting down arguments and every high thing that
> exalts itself against the knowledge of God, bringing

every thought into captivity to the obedience of
Christ. (2 Corinthians 10:4–5 NKJV)

As we come into agreement with heaven that God alone
reigns, the fear of the Lord will become evident in our lives.
Now as sons and daughters of the Most High, we will reap all
the benefits he has provided for his servants on earth. The chart
below represents a portion of the many benefits we receive as we
walk in the fear the Lord.

Scripture	Benefit
Psalm 103:11	God's love
Psalm 103:13	God's compassion
Psalm 85:9	Salvation
Psalm 111:10	Wisdom
Psalm 111:10	Good understanding
Psalm 112:1–2	Enjoyment in obeying God
Psalm 115:13	Blessings of God
Psalm 147:11	Pleasing unto God
Proverbs 1:7	Knowledge
Proverb 3:7–8	Healthy body
Proverbs 10:27	Lengthens your life
Proverbs 14:26	Protection for you and your children
Proverbs 15:16	Peace in all situations
Proverbs 23:17–18	A guaranteed future
Isaiah 33:6	His treasure

Teach me Your way, O Lord; I will walk in Your
truth; Unite my heart to fear Your name. (Psalm
86:11 NKJV)

Chapter 12

Approaching the Finish Line

For me to live is Christ, to die is gain. (Philippians 1:21 NIV)

Someone once said, "Everybody wants to go to heaven, but nobody wants to die." Call me naïve, but before I became born again, I had messed-up thoughts about death. I thought that when people died, they were buried in the ground to be there forever and ever. There were times when I would be all alone and I would allow myself to think about death. It was always overwhelming to me when I would think about never waking up and that nothing existed after death. It was not until I became born again that I understood about heaven and hell. It was exciting to know that there is life after death and that I had made the right decision. After I had chosen to be saved, I wanted to go to heaven. But I was not ready to go because I felt I was too young to die. Now, as I mature physically and spiritually, I understand that heaven is better than any place on earth.

Those of us who are watching for his appearance should look

forward to that great day. As born-again Christians, the focus should no longer be on our physical death because our new life is hidden in Christ. We have experienced death through Jesus Christ our Savior (Colossians 3:1–3). As we condition our spirits, we understand that the earth is not our permanent residence. We know that this place is merely a mission field to carry out the assignment God has given us to do.

> I have fought the good fight, I have finished the
> race, I have kept the faith. (2 Timothy 4:7 NIV)

Life is one huge race to be run by all who believe in Christ. The Bible says it is not given to the swift, nor the mighty, but to those who persevere till the end. The end of the race is approaching soon. How well did you run? Do you wish that you could do some things over? Are there some areas in your life where you are running short on faith? Has the light that was given to you at salvation become a source of comfort when trials come your way? Yes, a lot of questions have been thrown at you. But the good fight will continue long after you close this book.

Life for the believer is a race of endurance. To get to the finish line, you must keep God's word as the center of your life as you fight your way through by faith. As we see in 2 Timothy 4, Paul remained in faith throughout his relationship with God. He kept on the pathway that God chose for him to run. All that was left to do was to wait on the Lord. Paul knew he had finished his assignment and had accomplished the task at hand. We know from scriptures that Paul endured much persecution as he ran his race. However, being persecuted for having faith in God is not limited to the apostles of Christ. Second Timothy 3:12 (NKJV) says, "Yes, and all who desire to live godly in Christ Jesus will suffer persecution." No, we will not get to the end of this race without a fight.

Many of us will fall by the wayside by focusing more on the natural side of life rather than the spiritual side of life. Such things as fear, doubt, unbelief, anxiety, and worry will hinder your faith. Hebrews 11:27 (NIV) says, "By faith he [Moses] left Egypt, not fearing the king's anger; he persevered because he saw him who is invisible." It is faith in the invisible God that will keep you from running the race in vain. Without this kind of faith, you will not be able to please God. If faith in God is not present, whatever we do will be done according to our flesh.

We must make sure that we are running the race that God has set before us and not a race that we have chosen for ourselves to run. Remember Psalm 37:23 (NKJV) says, "The steps of a good man are ordered by the Lord." If we are to endure for the long haul, then we must keep our spiritual eyes open, carefully looking for the approaching finish line. Saints, you and I will know when that time comes, for we shall see the crown of righteousness that awaits us. Second Timothy 4:8 (NIV) says, "Now there is in store for me the crown of righteousness, which the Lord, the righteous Judge, will award to me on that day—and not only to me, but also to all who have longed for his appearing."

> In a moment, in the twinkling of an eye, at the
> last trumpet. For the trumpet will sound, and the

dead will be raised incorruptible, and we shall be
changed. (1 Corinthians 15:52 NKJV)

A snake periodically goes through a process called molting,
where he grows new skin and sheds his old skin. The exoskeleton
(the external skeleton) completely covers the outside of the body,
and the muscles inside of the snake adhere to it. It is hard and able
to protect the snake's body. When a snake gets ready to shed his
skin, he finds a hard surface like a rock to rub his head against
to start the shedding process, therefore losing the exoskeleton.
This process enables the snake to slide out of the old skin. The
shedding of the snake's skin is gradual enough to be caught on
film. We as spiritual beings are covered in our earthly bodies
while we live here on earth. But one day in the twinkling of an
eye, we will be changed. Unlike the lengthy process of the snake's
molting, our change will happen too quickly to catch on film.
The real you and I will be changed from a perishable being to an
imperishable being, ready to live on forever in our new bodies.

> Then I heard what sounded like a great multitude,
> like the roar of rushing waters and like loud peals
> of thunder, shouting: "Hallelujah! For our Lord
> God Almighty reigns. Let us rejoice and be glad
> and give him glory! For the wedding of the Lamb
> has come, and his bride has made herself ready.
> Fine linen, bright and clean, was given her to
> wear." [Fine linen stands for the righteous acts of
> God's holy people.] Then the angel said to me,
> "Write this: Blessed are those who are invited to

the wedding supper of the Lamb!" And he added, "These are the true words of God." (Revelation 19:6–9 NIV)

There is so much that goes into preparing for a wedding nowadays—things such as renting the venue or securing the church, reception hall, wedding rings, marriage license, wedding gown, bridesmaid gowns, tuxedos, food menu, the wedding cake, photographers, coordinators, hostesses, and ushers. I am sure I left some things off. But one day you and I will be a part of the grandest wedding celebration ever. For the Lamb that was slain, the time has come for him to receive his bride. The venue has been secured, and even the garment we will wear has been picked out for us. No detail has been overlooked for this occasion. This wedding will be out of this world. Yes, it will be in heaven. We are the bride to be, but unlike earthly weddings, our preparation is not about setting a date for the wedding, or planning bridal showers, bachelor parties, or a honeymoon. No, we prepare by living a holy and righteous life while on earth. As Jesus said in Matthew 4:4 (NKJV), "Man shall not live by bread alone, but by every word that proceeds out of the mouth of God." When we keep our lives spotless and without blemish before the Lord, God guarantees us a place at the marriage supper of the Lamb. For all the times that you and I wanted to give in and follow the world's lead, we will be glad that day that God kept us from making a fatal mistake.

I am reminded of the 1939 classic movie *The Wizard of Oz*, which was shown on television every year when I was growing up.

The main character, a young girl named Dorothy from Kansas, is caught in a tornado, hit on the head by a flying object, and knocked unconscious. She then dreams that her house has landed in a place called Oz, and thus begins the quest to get back home. The movie is filled with singing and laughter and some scary scenes. I always closed my eyes when I would see the wicked witch and the flying monkeys. There were times when it looked as if Dorothy was not going to get home. But toward the end of the movie, before she goes home, Dorothy is standing in Emerald City, clicking the heels of her ruby red shoes together and saying over and over, "There is no place like home. There is no place like home." No matter what you and I go through in this life's journey, we must decide in our hearts, sight unseen, there is no place like home—heaven.

> Now may the God of peace Himself sanctify you completely; and may your whole spirit, soul, and body be preserved blameless at the coming of our Lord Jesus Christ. He who calls you is faithful, who also will do it. (1 Thessalonians 5:23–24 NKJV)

Amen.